CHESAPEAKE BAY
DUCK HUNTING TALES

C.L. Marshall

THE History PRESS

Published by The History Press
Charleston, SC
www.historypress.net

Front cover, background: Canada geese sit tight, conserving energy during a frigid January afternoon, in a snow-covered Chestertown field. *Paul Bramble Photography*; *top, right*: Hope Barroll poses with his dog Gilly in preparation for another day in the salt marshes. *Courtesy Saxis Island Museum*; *top, left*: Bucca hauls in a fat redhead drake from the shallow waters of the upper Chesapeake. *Paul Bramble Photography*.

First published 2016

Manufactured in the United States

ISBN 978.1.46713.728.7

Library of Congress Control Number: 2016945908

A book's dedication usually denotes a few individuals who made an impression on the writer. It calls out those who provided inspiration, a kick in the ass or compassion when any is needed. Well, in my life, that is a long list. In no particular order, I'd like to thank my family, friends, Maker's Mark Distillery and various farmers across the Mid-Atlantic area for making my stories come alive on these few pages.

CONTENTS

Contents

PREFACE

It was a simple enough conversation. Billy Smith and I were each sitting on painted five-gallon buckets, counting our birds to make sure we weren't over the limit. The ducks had flown early and provided us with twenty minutes of fast and furious shooting. The sun had yet to peek over the horizon. My dog had been in the water the whole time and still had much work to do. Billy said that someone should write a book about stuff like what we had just experienced. I thought that exploits such as these would certainly land us both in jail. We tabled the idea.

Though that conversation took place long ago, the thought of putting a book together was always in the back of my mind. As I reviewed hunting logs from past years, I set the process in motion. I've been blessed to share blinds

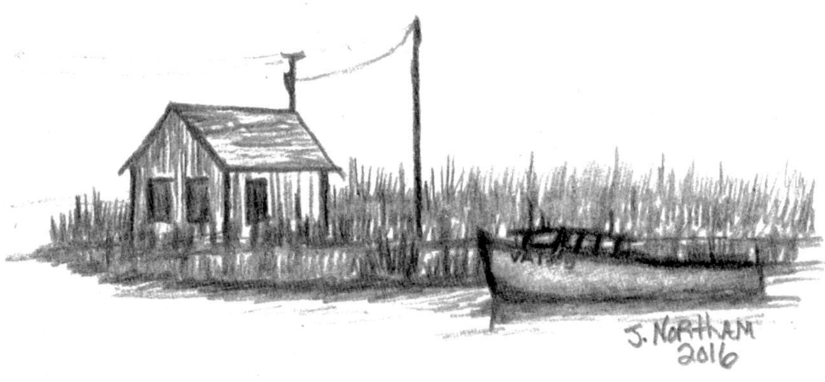

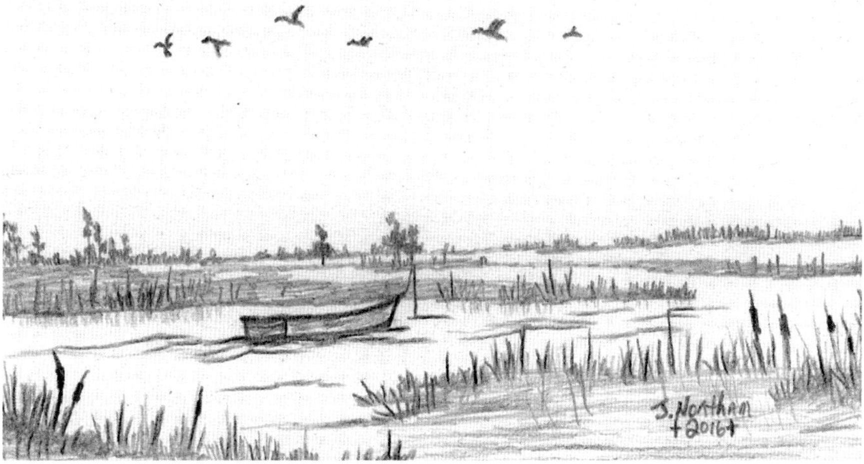

with folks from all walks of life. The stories within provide a mere glimpse into the relationships that I've forged with each. I'm eternally grateful for all of them. These bonds go far beyond the blind.

These stories are gleaned from over forty years of chasing waterfowl in the Chesapeake Bay and its tributaries. Some of the techniques used may be questionable to some. Over the years, the "old ways" of harvesting waterfowl have given way to legally flooding mature grain plots, barrel stickers and boats with light bars piercing the night. Given the legislation, tax breaks and legal loopholes provided by the law of today, great advantage is provided to those with land and money to donate under the guise of "habitat management" or "habitat restoration." Regardless of regulation changes, the end result is the same for the ducks. One difference is the costs to get the grain in the water. Another difference is in the eyes of the law. Such practices have undoubtedly changed the face of hunting on the Eastern Flyway.

This collection of stories is not so much about the actual hunting as it is about the people and events involved in the hunting experience. The actual pulling of the trigger is not the main reason many of us hunt. Some like the preparation, others love the dog work and still others go for the natural surroundings.

Many go because it is part of who we are. For me, it's bred into my soul. I've tried to quit it, but I always come back to it. No barrel stickers or light bars for me. It's old school; it's Saxis Island style.

Acknowledgements

Without the following individuals, this book would not have been possible. I'd like to thank each for his or her contributions in making this book a reality.

Paul Bramble Photography
Saxis Island Museum
Joyce Northam, artwork
Esther Troast
Carroll Lee's Decoys

A DAY REMEMBERED

Growing up as a duck hunter near Saxis Island, there are two things that we'd look forward to: ice and a hard northeast wind. In an area we called "the backside," this combination meant that as the tide rose, the hard wind would push the ice away from the bank. In search of food and open water, both local and newly arriving waterfowl would find their way to this ever-expanding strip of available habitat.

It was a scenario that we'd played out numerous times, and we knew the outcome as we were loading gear the night before—or so we thought.

It's a hunting style that is not for the faint hearted or the ill prepared. Breaking ice is hard on hulls, lower units and props. Ice up to four inches thick would be busted out of the ramp just to get the boats in the water. On this day, three boats of hearty souls would "break out" toward various hunting locations that had been good to us over the past years. Things looked promising.

Progress through the ice was slow as we followed the tracks cut through the ice the day before. The crunching, grinding sound made by the conflict of bay ice verses the hull of the twenty-foot Gaskill scow would certainly frighten the uninitiated. We longed for it. We dreamed about days like this. Instinctually, we made our way out of the harbor toward the Free School marsh knowing that we'd find open water along the bank and more unencumbered travel. This was a game we had played before.

My gunning partner, Paige Linton, and I headed for a spot we had dubbed Cambodia, named as much for the bushing, composed of bamboo stalks and leaves, as for the incredible amount of shooting that erupted from there

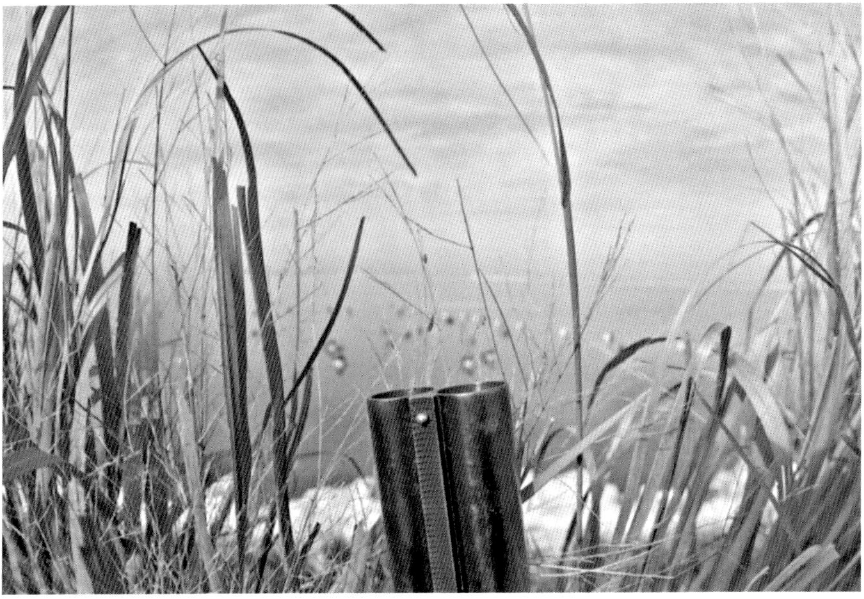

Continually hunted for over forty years, Cambodia was the site of many lasting memories. This vantage point was shared by many over the years. *Paul Bramble photo.*

on a regular basis. The blind had been positioned such that it would be the perfect perch on days like this. It was of outstanding construction. With the wind at our back, the caulked, enclosed plywood hut would be warm and dry. Paige's father, Frank, had claimed the spot some thirty years ago, and it had been hunted continually since that day.

The only evidence of the rising sun was the lightening hues of gray. Its rays were muted by overcast skies. Making our way slowly in compromised light, we finally reached Cambodia, and the other two skiffs kept on down below. With a wave, they were on their way, and we set about tying our rig. Because the birds were desperate for open water and food, big spreads were not required. We set half a dozen geese downwind, with eight or so black ducks and a pair of pintails just inside and upwind from the geese. A dozen and a half cans and blackheads were placed just right of the blind. The ribbon of water bordering the marsh had widened to twenty or so yards. The wind picked up to twenty knots. Daylight came late on this day.

Paige stepped out on the ice crusted marsh, and I handed him our gear, minus my shotgun, from the boat. He diligently began to make the blind ready for action. I eased the boat off the marsh and headed upwind to hide it in a little gut about one hundred yards away. Just below the waterline, I was able to sink my pole, caught a half hitch with the frozen bow line and backed it up just for good measure with the anchor. This was not the day to lose the boat. Uncasing and loading my gun, I began the walk back to the blind as Paige started the day with a fat single mallard drake. He had another pair of ten-point ducks before I got in the box. It was on.

We worked on a steady shoot of dabblers as the tide continued to rise. As the birds came in singles and pairs, we quickly made a nice pile. Being selective, we passed on numerous shots at small ducks. We wanted to make the day last. As the tide got higher, the flight of puddle ducks slowed, and shots of diving ducks began to increase dramatically. We were interested in big ducks, and they were willing. Our barrels were as hot as the charcoal grill warming our coffee and grilled pork chop sandwiches. The divers were coming in bigger bunches, with one toll of canvasbacks numbering well over one hundred. It was a helluva day.

The other two boats that broke out with us had already headed in. We thought it a bit odd for them to be going back in so early. We assumed correctly that they had enjoyed the same hunting success that we were experiencing. But that day, lives were changed forever.

Paige and I hunted together frequently. At the time, I had a Chesapeake named Butler, and Paige was running a blockheaded black lab named Mojo. Aside from breed, the two dogs were much the same. Both were outstanding gun dogs—steady to the shot, excellent noses and with unparalleled drives to please. Both were also alpha males and would fight each other to the death. In one incident, Mojo was inside Paige's car, and Butler was outside of it. Trying to get at Butler, Mojo actually bit the back window of Paige's Caprice with such force that it broke the glass. Needless to say, they never were able to hunt together.

Most hunters would have left the dogs at home on days like this. But Butler wasn't most dogs. He worked steadily all morning, losing the occasional cripple under the ice. He was no different from us. He loved to duck hunt, he loved to retrieve, and today he was in his element. His thick coat covered in ice, he would occasionally open the blind door with his nose, smelling what we were warming on the grill and wanting his share. He got it; he'd certainly earned it.

We decided to pack it in. We picked up the decoys and loaded the gear, and very soon, we were underway. We left a two-man limit of "show ducks" on the seat. Extras were stowed in a white poly feed bag. The tide had turned to outgoing. The tracks that our fellow hunters had made closed. Ice from up the creek had begun to slowly, powerfully retreat with the current. The ribbon of water under the bank closed quickly, and we were forced to slowly crunch our way back toward the dock.

As we made our way closer to the harbor, the scene became increasingly confusing. It became even more difficult to handle as we made the final turn toward the boat ramp. The white poly bag was eased over stern and tossed under the dock in a pile of ice. It blended in perfectly and would be easily retrieved at a later time. The mood quickly turned serious when we stepped on the dock and learned what had unfolded within the other group. One of our friends, Orlen Trader, and been the victim of an unfortunate accident that claimed his life.

Each time I pass by that point jutting out into shallow waters of the bay where this tragic event occurred, I can't help but think of Orlen. I think of the effect that he had on us while he was with us and of the effect he's had on us since he left. His Herter's decoys are well cared for and still in use, his name still inscribed on their bottoms in black permanent marker.

Though Orlen was a couple years younger, I'd worked with him at the crab house. He'd fished crab pots with me. He was a friend. One hot summer day, he rode with me to Buck Kambarn's in Chincoteague to pick up my crabbing skiff with a new Johnson seventy-horsepower outboard. Two gallons of copper paint were set between us on the bench seat of my '72 Chevy Stepside pickup. We rear ended a garbage truck on Queen Sound bridge. The paint cans flew from the seat and smashed against the dash with such force that the lids come off and the paint covered us. Once we ascertained that we were OK following the crash, we scurried out of the passenger side window. Covered in that paint, onlookers thought we were bleeding profusely and ran to offer assistance. While I watched my truck and boat burn in the fire the crash resulted in, Orlen was preoccupied with cleaning the paint stains off his new Pony high-top sneakers.

That day we were lucky.

On this day, we were not.

THREE'S A CHARM FOR THE DUKE

We waited in the truck, sipping hot coffee and nibbling at sausage biscuits as sunlight slowly gave view to the ice floes drifting by in the swift-running Pocomoke River current. Last night's trip to Wright's Butchery had slowed our morning activity but not our desire. We were just taking our time, as step one of the "trifecta" for my college buddy had been completed the previous afternoon.

An old college roommate from Germantown, Maryland, Ed "the Duke" Snider, had made the trip down to hunt the weekend with me. Both duck and deer hunting had been good, and I wanted to get him on the scoreboard on both accounts. A goose would complete the Eastern Shore Slam. He'd shown up on Friday afternoon just after lunch. After cordial greetings and unpacking, we immediately headed for the deer stand. Ed had been deer hunting in suburbia for a couple years with limited success. Friday afternoon's hunt looked promising from the beginning, as we pushed three does out of the field walking to the stand. Once in the stand, we had a steady stream of yearlings and small does amble in and out of the woods. We had time, and the odds were good that a decent buck would poke his head out. Whether Ed would close the deal remained to be seen.

It was refreshing to see such excitement in the eyes of a fellow hunter. This was all new for him. As we sat in the two-man box stand, we watched four does feed greedily on the brassica that I'd planted in late August. Bursting out of the woods on the east side of the field in a full trot, the beamy six-pointer showed no real interest in the does. He was, however, interested in dinner. The Duke brought his gun up on command but couldn't find the deer in the scope. I managed to stop him at 182 yards, offering a perfect broadside shot. Ed found him in the scope. Calming himself, he squeezed off a round, and the deer collapsed. When he turned to me with this huge grin on his face, I saw his joy in finally bagging his first buck. It was also easy to see the blood trickling down the bridge of his nose. Concentrating on aim, controlled breathing and the shot, Ed had allowed the scope to bite him. He had no idea of the injury until I showed him the picture on my phone, just prior to broadcasting it to the full Sigma Pi brotherhood. The first step in our trifecta had been achieved. With a nice deer down, we were on our way to the butcher. There we'd remain for a couple hours, sipping cold beer and rehashing Ed's adventure with Siloam's finest.

The cold snap had just started, and with temperatures dropping to single digits for the next few days, access to open water would become limited. The smaller tributaries and ponds had already frozen. The forecast for the weekend called for light snow, winds increasing to twenty miles per hour from the northeast and ducks. If there was ever a day made for shooting divers on the Pocomoke Sound, this would be the one. In limited visibility, we launched the skiff and picked our way through the ice to open water just inside the mouth of the Pocomoke River. The first snowflakes of the day began to fall. The newly falling snow, the wind and ebbing tide would all work in our favor.

Setting up with the wind off the port bow, Ed, my son Parker and I would be afforded right-to-left decoying shots. Parker drove the push pole into the mud, and his half hitch drew the bow tight to the marsh. I pitched the anchor up on the marsh and pulled the stern as close as possible to the bank. The outboard was lowered, and the lower unit pegged the skiff in place. As we were popping up our blind, we began to look for approaching birds. We spotted our first visitors as they buzzed past William's Point. Making their way toward Double Ditches, they followed the path laid by many before them. Following the bank northward toward the river, they spotted our spread. The hurtling mass of feathered fury cut across the decoys at warp speed. On the second pass, the knot of bluebills caught the wind in their cupped wings and slowed greatly over the decoys. Five of the fifteen pitched while the balance swung around for another pass. They seemed content; we waited on the swing.

Time slowed as the remaining ten twisted and darted like puppets coming to the decoys. The incoming were dealt with first, our attention then turning to picking off those rising from the water one by one. Our subsequent

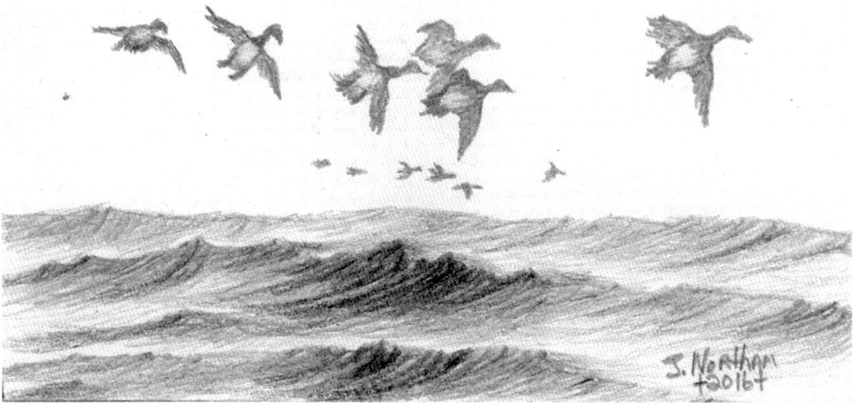

customers came as a pair. The shot was called on the first pass. Ed rolled his out cleanly; seated in the center, I held tight. As Parker pulled on the drake canvasback, the push pole that he had tied the bow to caught part of the wad, relieving it of a semicircular swath of oak. The second shot found its mark, sending the bird cart wheeling into the bank. The birds continued to cooperate throughout the morning. Flock after flock allowed us access to the show of a lifetime. It's one that we'll never forget.

The third and final leg of the trifecta consisted of a successful goose hunt. Stopping off at Royal Farms for a box of fried chicken, a few Red Bulls and a new tin of Copenhagen, we prepared for our afternoon wild goose hunt. A dozen or so Bud Lights were hidden under the ice in the Yeti cooler for the post-hunt celebration. Dropping the boat off at the house, we loaded the truck with three dozen full-body goose decoys and the same amount of shell decoys. In short order, we headed for the field. The past twenty-four hours must have been a blur for a fellow from Germantown. He'd been ushered to a tree stand where he saw more deer than he'd seen in his life and shot a worthy buck. Shortly thereafter, he was drinking beer with Siloam's finest at a butcher shop in the middle of nowhere. He'd risen early, a bit dazed and confused, to experience bluebill shooting at its finest. Now he lay on his back with his face obscured by bean stalks listening to us coax geese toward the decoys. We had done our fair share of living over the last day.

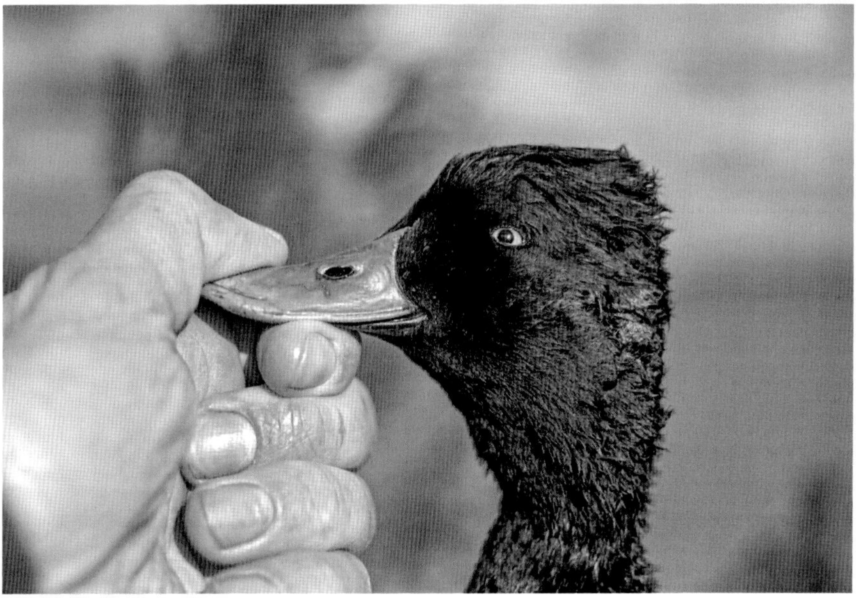

With the morning sun highlighting the iridescent coloring of their black heads, scaup are a beautiful species to behold. *Paul Bramble photo.*

Cold weather and moisture had the geese using a low-lying soybean field just across the river. This afternoon, the geese had other plans. The first two flocks just wouldn't finish. Several others simply had no interest. A willing single made the commitment from a half mile away. Little calling was required to close the deal. Tremendous patience was required as the goose hung in the air like a landing Boeing 747. We let Duke see the whole show, not calling the shot until the goose had let his landing gear down and begun to "back pedal" into the decoys. She was dispatched cleanly on Duke's second shot, completing his trifecta.

In less than thirty-six hours, we had accomplished what some strive a lifetime to achieve. Luck had some part in it, but luck tends to ultimately find those who work hard. There is no mistake that we put in the work on that weekend. The joy of sharing such experiences makes all the hard work worthwhile.

AN INNOCENT MAN

In my hunting career, there is something that I've been called only once. The words "innocent man" never really seemed to fit my hunting style during the early years of my hunting career. Yet from the bench of the highest court in the region, that is exactly what I was labeled.

How we got to that point makes for an interesting story.

We'd been under the influence of a high-pressure system for nearly ten days. The balmy weather was more conducive to fishing than duck hunting, but it was Thanksgiving. There were a few birds around, and any time that I could hunt with my two sons, it was bound to be a good trip. We looked forward to the day.

The flurry of activity in the predawn hours was typical. Fortunately, my boys are fairly self-sufficient when it comes to hunting and had all their gear together, in good condition and properly stowed in the skiff. After a quick inventory check, we were off to Royal Farms to get coffee, snacks and a little fuel.

Butch and Anthony Thomas were planning on going as well. They'd be hunting just down the creek from us at a well-hidden spot we called "Our Blind." Our Blind had been stuck by a fellow who hunted with us for a couple years. Though a good hunter, his disposition wasn't one that jived with our style of hunting, and we decided to part ways. We claimed the blind as ours.

Since my sons and I had the longest run, we launched first. My two boys, our golden retriever Gunner and I eagerly jumped aboard, and we were off. A rising tide, calm winds and a waning Gibbous moon made the ride through the darkness quite enjoyable. The sound and feel of the four stroke–powered fiberglass hull slicing through my home waters made for a very peaceful feeling. Behind me a couple hundred yards, I could see the bow lights of Anthony's skiff and, by their attitude, that he was throttling up. I was looking forward to the morning's hunt.

Though the weather was calm, the truth is we'd been hammering the teal and black ducks for weeks. Between trips, we'd been doing what was required to ensure good hunting. Keeping the ducks around was beneficial for all of us. This cat-and-mouse game with the local law had been going on for years. It was inevitable how it would end.

With my usual diligence, I made my way up the creek. Casting a light up Marsh Market road to check for trucks or boats, I found that it was empty. The beams I shot up in the typical hiding places for boats on the way up the creek found that they, too, were vacant. I always checked the edges of the marsh, especially on this rising tide, to check for the wash made by a boat's wake clinging to the reedy shore line, and there was none. Nor was there the foam trail that a wake will leave along the shoreline. Things were looking good. It appeared that we would be alone up the creek this morning.

The way things were, we didn't need to tie a big rig. Six to eight decoys were usually enough. Like clockwork the birds began to show up just at legal shooting time. I let the boys shoot, and I worked the dog. On this day, very few flew, and by 7:30 a.m., we had only three teal. The bag really didn't matter. The boys had shot a bunch, and Gunner had done his job well. Our friends down the creek from us were pounding on them. On this still morning, a steady salvo from Our Blind meant that they were having a very good day.

As we were thinking about taking up, I placed a call to Anthony. He confirmed our suspicion and acknowledged that he had them piled up. Thinking that our constant shooting on such a calm day might draw the interest of locals, other hunters or more importantly "the man," I suggested that he drop some of his ducks off to us prior to coming to the dock. We certainly didn't want to show up at the dock over the limit. He agreed, and in a few minutes, he picked up and made the run up the creek to us. He pulled alongside the bank and cut his motor. We chatted about his good hunt, and he tossed a dozen or so teal on the bank in front of the blind.

That's when all hell broke loose.

From just behind the blind came one officer of the law. From up the creek came a boat with two more. They positioned their sea foam–colored Bay Raider such that neither Anthony nor I could make a run for it—not that we would. The thought didn't cross our minds. We just waited to see what was about to happen.

After considerable discussion, I was charged with possession of untagged migratory fowl, possession of illegally taken waterfowl and whatever else they could pile on. Citations were issued to me, and we were free to go. Anthony and Butch were required to return to Our Blind with the officers so pictures could be taken of the crime scene. As the illegally taken fowl was spread on the bow of Anthony's olive drab Southern Skimmer, his yellow lab Max jumped right up there and posed for the picture like he'd done it a few times before. Fact is, he had.

Several months later, our date in Norfolk federal court had arrived. We sat among the rapists in chains and criminals in orange jumpsuits awaiting our trial on duck hunting charges. It was an eye-opening experience. I was called first, and the officers did an adequately accurate job in detailing the events of that morning. I offered a few corrections from my perspective, pleaded guilty and took my punishment. It wasn't my first violation, and they stuck it to me pretty good. A fine, a year in the penalty box and a short probationary period following reinstatement seemed to satisfy the U.S. government. I, on the other hand, wasn't too pleased.

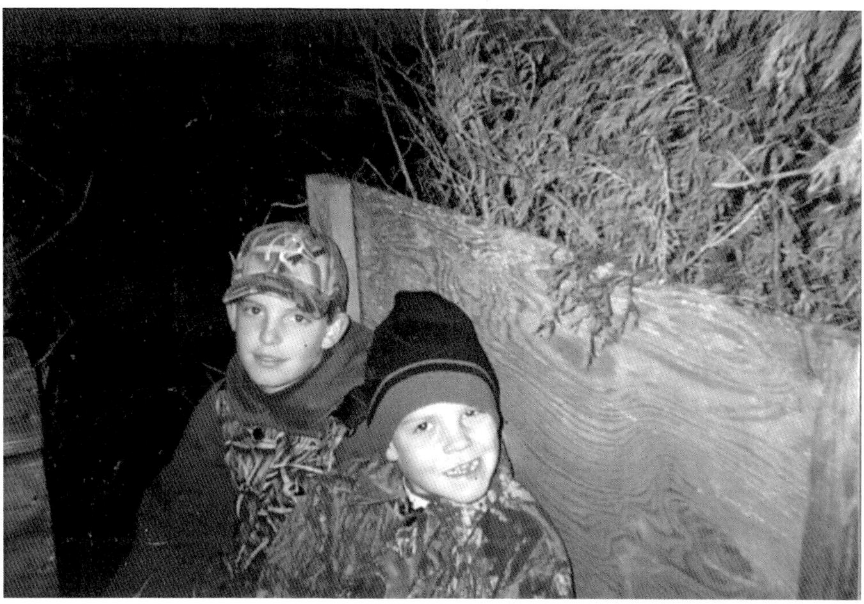

My two boys, Hunter and Parker, sit awaiting the first shot of the day at the Spank Box. We've had many good sandwiches there waiting for legal shooting time. *C.L. Marshall photo.*

The Thomases, both Anthony and his father, were tried at the same time. They explained their version of things, how the ducks just kept coming, how they couldn't resist the urge to keep shooting and how they lost track of the number of birds downed in all the excitement. They also corroborated their part in my situation.

Then the unexpected happened. The judge was a duck hunter and said he could see how, in the excitement, something like this could happen and that the penalties that the prosecution was looking for in this case were absurd. Though he was sympathetic to the cause, he was bound by duty to find them guilty with a fine of $500 apiece. Then things got really weird. He imposed an additional fine of $250 each. As he did this, he pointed to me and claimed the extra $250 was, and I quote, "for getting an innocent man in trouble." Butch muttered that the only time I was innocent was shortly after my birth. The judge chuckled a bit and closed the case with a slap of his gavel.

I won't let them forget it, and they won't let me forget their additional expense.

ASSAULT AND BATTERY

The noise made by the twenty-five geese on their first pass was pleasing. From great altitude, they had decided that the field was acceptable, and our decoy spread had provided added enticement. Once one has experienced the sound made by the collision of wind and the wings of a flock of Canada geese, it quickly becomes addictive. It will consume you until you hear it again and again.

Four of us waited in well-concealed layout blinds for them to get right. Four more men waited in warm trucks sipping coffee for their turn in the blinds. They watched from a distance of two hundred yards as these twenty-five geese finished their turn, lost altitude and began a low approach to the decoys. The calling and coaxing was over now. They'd made their decision, and their approach was guided by only a few soft clucks and moans. Those in the front began a backward motion with their wings to slow their approach as their feet went down. Those in the back didn't quite get the message. They piled up just behind the leaders and then slid both left and right of those in front. Now they were at twenty-five yards, and we rose to handle our business.

Five lay in the snow with two more limping off. Up and out of the layout, the trek to retrieve the two attempted escapees ended quickly. While we were standing in the decoys attempting to get our spread back in order, a single just wouldn't take no for an answer. It was added to the pile, and the text was sent for crew number two to roll in. In short order, they came across the frozen field in my old 1992 Chevy Blazer. Having been well educated in

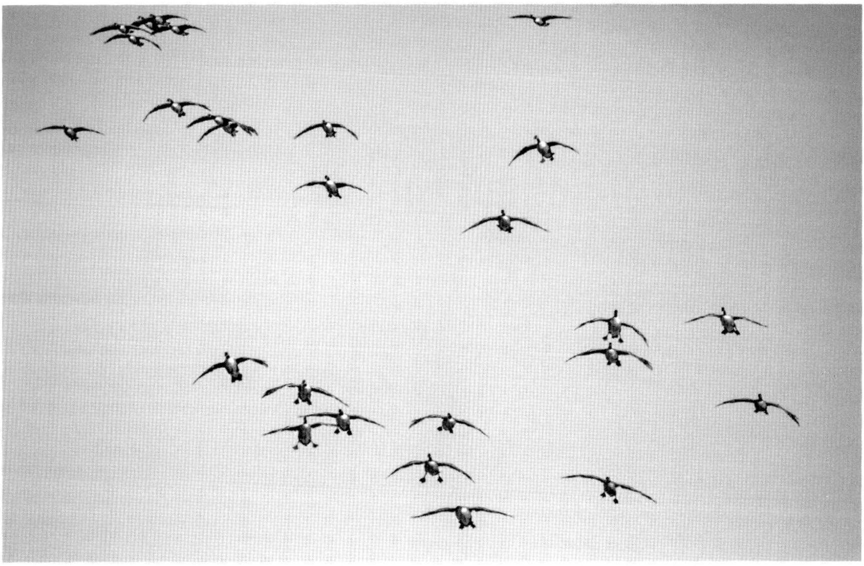

There is no sound as unique as that made by the collision of wind and the wings of a flock of Canada geese. It can become quite addictive. *Paul Bramble photo.*

the federal requirements concerning possession limits, transferring wildfowl, tagging and all that goes with it, I tossed the eight geese through the broken back window into the back of the SUV. The retractable back window had been broken by a decoy weight two weeks prior. With hunting season winding down quickly, it was low on the priority list of things to get done.

The four of us made our way out of the field as the others made ready for the action that was sure to come. Taking our place along the tree line, we positioned our truck so that we could see how our comrades would fare. All the usual suspects were present. Bobby Graves, David Graham, Greg East and I had done our job nicely. It wasn't until the second Bud Light Lime was cracked that the foursome of our three sons and one of their friends had their first opportunity. Three of the four geese stayed behind, and we toasted their good work.

Relatively quickly, the junior hunters' work totaled six. We were planning on steamed oysters and clams, as well as some goose fajitas, back at the shop after the hunt. East decided that he'd head back and get things cooking while the rest of us got things packed up. Most likely, the kids would be finished shortly. With that decision made, we waited for a break in the action and swooped into their spread with the Blazer, tossing their six into the back of the truck with our geese. East was to take the Blazer, with the geese in the back, to the shop. With a broken driver's seat, broken back window and a heater that didn't work, the SUV took off toward Pocomoke. Though East was a little nervous about driving such a "relic" of a vehicle, we reassured him that he'd be OK, provided he wasn't stopped by the game warden with all those geese in the back. We would wait for the youths to claim their other two geese and be along soon. With East nervously trekking back toward the shop, we settled into the cold Ford truck for what we hoped would be a short wait.

It didn't take long, as six geese lifted off the river, barely cleared the tall loblolly pines and committed to the decoys. Three shots rang out, and two geese fell. It was pretty work. Cleanup and decoy retrieval went very quickly. It's amazing how fast things can get done on a cold day with the promise of hot steamed seafood on the horizon. It wasn't until we arrived back at the shop that we found out about the "real" excitement for the day.

Apparently, as East was heading back toward Pocomoke, there was some commotion in the back of the truck. Looking in the rear view mirror, East saw a gander, neck erect, staring at the back of his head. It seemed the goose had plenty of life left in him and wanted nothing to do with the driver or the truck. Not the calmest person in a crisis, East began to scream at the goose while pushing it away with his right hand. With that, the goose started to wreak havoc inside the truck. East fought valiantly to maintain control of

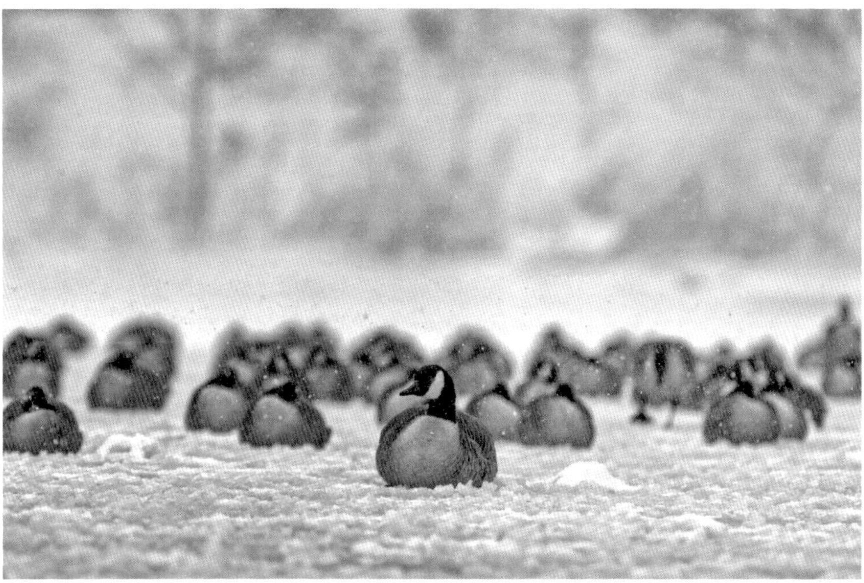

On cold, windy, snowy days, geese tend to huddle on the ground. Adding sleeper decoys can lead to increased success. *Paul Bramble photo.*

the truck while keeping the goose at bay. Having had enough of the driver and the ride, the goose made its way out of the back of the truck through the broken window. After a couple rolls on the asphalt, the goose stood erect on the road as it gathered its wits about it. Quickly, it was aloft, escaping the fate of its feathered friends that remained in the back of the Blazer. It was that goose's lucky day.

As we arrived back at the shop, one short of a limit, we could see the poor fellow sitting on a stool, watching the oysters steam. It was easy to see how visibly shaken he was by the ordeal. He had done his job, although we were bound to hear about it all night. The first of the oysters were coming off the steamer just as we got our gear stowed. With the addition of more Bud Light Lime and some Maker's Mark, the story of the harassment by the goose turned into a full-fledged assault.

Our hunt and the opportunity to share it with our sons was clearly the most valued part of that day. But the goose assaulting East and then fleeing through the broken window—that was priceless.

BARRIER ISLAND MOONSHINE

We lay silently, surrounded by the sounds of nature as dozens of ducks circled overhead. The chatty sound of their feeding call seemed to fade and intensify as the mallards made yet another circling maneuver. Four black ducks had no interest in circling. Coming in low over the needle grass, they sat down neatly by the exposed tires. They knew exactly what they were there for. We just sat and waited.

There was no need to worry about competition from other hunters. The moon was near full, and any other hunters or watermen who had been out on this afternoon had long since gone home to dinner. From our vantage point, we could plainly see the silhouettes of black ducks, fat mallards, pesky little teals and sprig tails basking in the moonlight. The ambient light from the Wallops Island launch facility and the clear, crisp full winter moon made the wait much more tolerable than on past nights.

As it neared ten o'clock, we could see a steady stream of cars traveling on the Chincoteague causeway. It seemed incredibly busy for a Tuesday night. The clear and cold weather provided for excellent visibility. The navigational beacons of the surrounding bays blinked a regular beat. We whispered and wondered about the numerous cars that ventured down the Arbuckle Neck road, each sitting there for a few minutes before turning to leave. One such visitor extinguished his lights and sat for over an hour. Though it would be impossible for this visitor to walk to our nicely hidden spot, there was a sign of relief when the lights came back on and tail lights signaled his departure.

Though we looked calm on the exterior, our heads were on swivels during the first few minutes of our hunt. Nervously watching, listening and making certain that we were indeed alone on this barrier island was priority number one. While the nervousness never really went away, it was soon replaced by a calmer, more restful demeanor. There was no worry that homeowners or NASA personnel would hear our shooting due to the offshore direction of the increasing breeze. Temperatures nearing freezing at this hour of night would certainly keep most homeowners swaddled on the sofa. We were the only fools who would be on this desolate stretch of beach on this night. With these fears allayed, we settled in for the night.

In spite of the cold northwest wind, now gusting at fifteen miles per hour, the sound of crashing waves on the beach just one hundred yards away was soothing. Warm and comfy in our brushed-up layout blinds, we sat semi-erect, sipping coffee and watching the wildlife show. Upon our arrival just an hour ago, we had jumped over one hundred out of this little seaside pond. They had just started returning thirty minutes ago. Their shapes twisted and darted and then disappeared momentarily as they passed the muddy banks of the pond, reappearing as a series of silhouettes pushing Vs through the still water.

We planned our first shot for 10:30 p.m. We would then shoot again every fifteen minutes thereafter until we had the ducks that we needed. By employing this method, the number and frequency of shots would be greatly diminished, drawing less attention to our illicit activities. There would be no wing shooting. When the time came, we would simply slide our guns to our shoulders and be ready to fire. Three or more birds should be aligned prior to calling the shot. My partner and I had done this before. Planning and conversation weren't really that necessary anymore. A simple "Ready?" followed by "Yep" in hushed voices would immediately be followed by six or more shots in rapid succession. Visible cripples would be capped. The results of our work would be blown to the downwind side of the pond for retrieval later.

As the appointed time neared, the pond populated quickly. Our adrenaline began to slowly build in anticipation of the pending action. Glancing at my watch, I cleared my throat to get my partner's attention. A simple nod put the series of events in motion. The two of us moved in unison as partners in a dance that had been performed by our fathers, grandfathers and many others in our lineage. With our old Remingtons silently shouldered, the usual commands were given and received. The eruption of gunfire that this initiated caught the thirty puddle ducks surrounding the two corn-filled tires by surprise. The first shots were each directed at a mass of feeding fowl. At a distance of twenty-five yards, our patterns were uniform and tight, each about fourteen inches in diameter, cutting a swath through the middle of the flock. Second shots were squeezed off quickly into the same mass of feathers. Neither of us opted for a third short. The muzzle flashes had caused us to temporarily lose visual contact with our targets. There was no need to rush things. We had all night.

Two follow-up shots were required to handle the pair of cripples that we could see. Calmly, we settled back into our hiding spots, whispering to each other our guesses on how many we took. This scenario played out three times over the course of the evening, each at the appointed time. There were no decoys to worry about picking up. Leisurely, we emptied the two burlap sacks of yellow acorns in and around the two tires we'd set in the shallow pond over the summer as the birds continued to try to fall in the water. Our shooting was over; it was time to pick up our stuff and blend back in with civilization. For nearly three hours, we'd lived in time long since gone, fully aware of the risk we were taking. Such events are seldom spoken about outside certain circles.

Using the red-light feature of our headlamps, we each took a now empty sack bag and began to pick up the fruits of our labor. It didn't take long, as the northwest wind had piled up the dead along the boundary of the pond. Pick up went relatively easy, despite a couple brief chases for undead birds across the sandy-bottomed pond. Firm footing and good visibility aided in ending these chases quickly. The mallards, gadwalls, teals and pintails were the easiest to find. Picking up black ducks on the edge of a marsh pond under the full moon requires a certain finesse.

The trek back to the boat wasn't a long one and was made a bit easier by replacing the weight of the corn we hauled in with the weight of our kill on the way out. As midnight approached, we made it back to the skiff. Placing our blind and sacks laden with fowl in the bow section of the skiff, we quickly stowed the anchor and idled unlit through the labyrinth of guts and ditches back to our trucks. As we walked to our trucks, the moonlight allowed us to survey the situation. All looked as it should. The boat was quickly tied as my partner stepped out on the hard. Deliberately, I tossed the layout blinds and sacks loaded with birds out of the skiff, and they were quickly deposited in the back of the pickup. Stepping out with the guns in hand, I simply dropped them in the backseat of the truck, removed my warm camo gear and tossed them over the guns. Seated now in the warmth of the truck and dressed like civilians, we eased away from the boat. We'd pick it up later in the coming day to avoid additional suspicion.

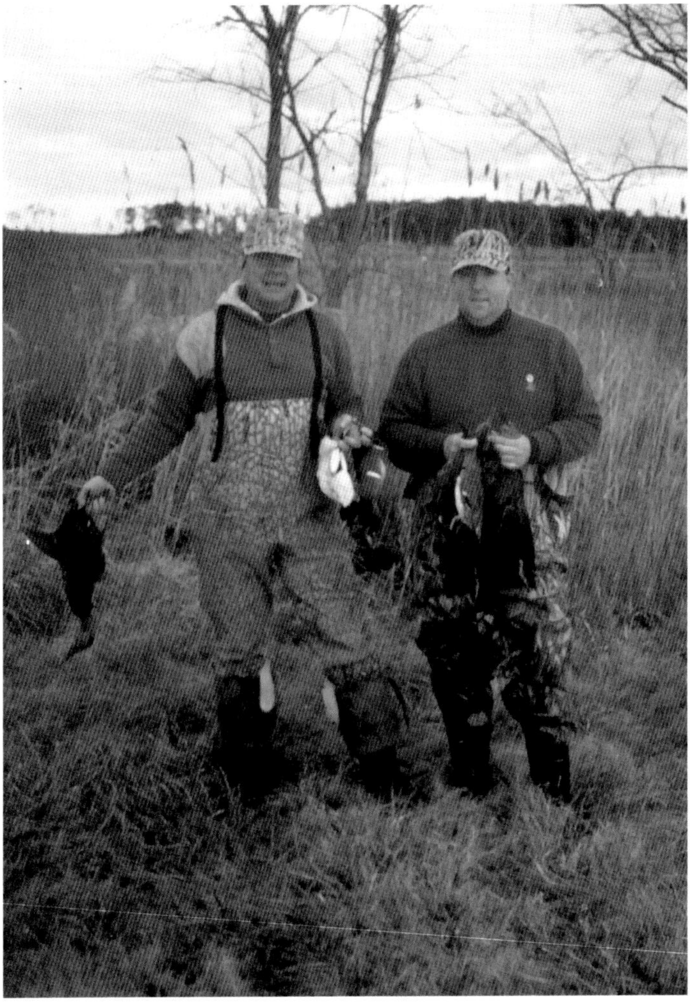

Paige Linton (left) and I pose for a rare picture after a successful morning's hunt at Cambodia. Blacks, teal and a handful of divers made for a great hunt on this day. *Arnold Spence photo.*

Stopping at the nearest convenience store for a box of fried chicken and a tin of Copenhagen, we spoke briefly about the events we had just shared. It couldn't have gone much better. The folks over home would have the ducks they needed for the Christmas holiday.

Looking just across the street, Chattie's Bar was still open. We decided to end our night with a good, strong bourbon to cap off our adventures. All was right with the world.

BEGINNINGS AND ENDINGS

Sitting in the box at Piney Hammocks with a strong northwest wind off my left shoulder, I didn't even notice the pair of black ducks that had pitched in the chaffy-bottomed cove to my left. There was no telling just how long they'd been there or how long it had taken the wind to bring them to the eight black duck decoys that I'd haphazardly tossed over about an hour ago. It was the last day of the season, and I was lost in reflection about the season's ending and the events of this day. This was a season whose end couldn't come soon enough.

For a duck hunter, there is nothing quite like the optimism of a new season. Regardless of what happened last year, or the number of birds killed, the opportunity to start anew is always inspiring. Things start to get moving in September, when the wood duck and teal decoys are pulled out and washed. Knots are retied and weights checked while thoughts of dancing and darting wood ducks fill my mind. Scouting missions double as rock fishing trips. These jaunts provide a short list of things that must be repaired before gunning begins. The balance of the decoys is pulled out, and though they went into storage in good working order, they are checked again prior to being packed into the totes that they'll occupy for the next ninety days. The usual media searches are made, but I know the outcome prior to receiving the results. "Another record year!," "More Ducks than Ever," "Tremendous Amount of Ducks Headed Your Way" are the usual calls to action. The fact is, however, that these headlines are designed more for their advertisers' bottom lines than our gunning sacks.

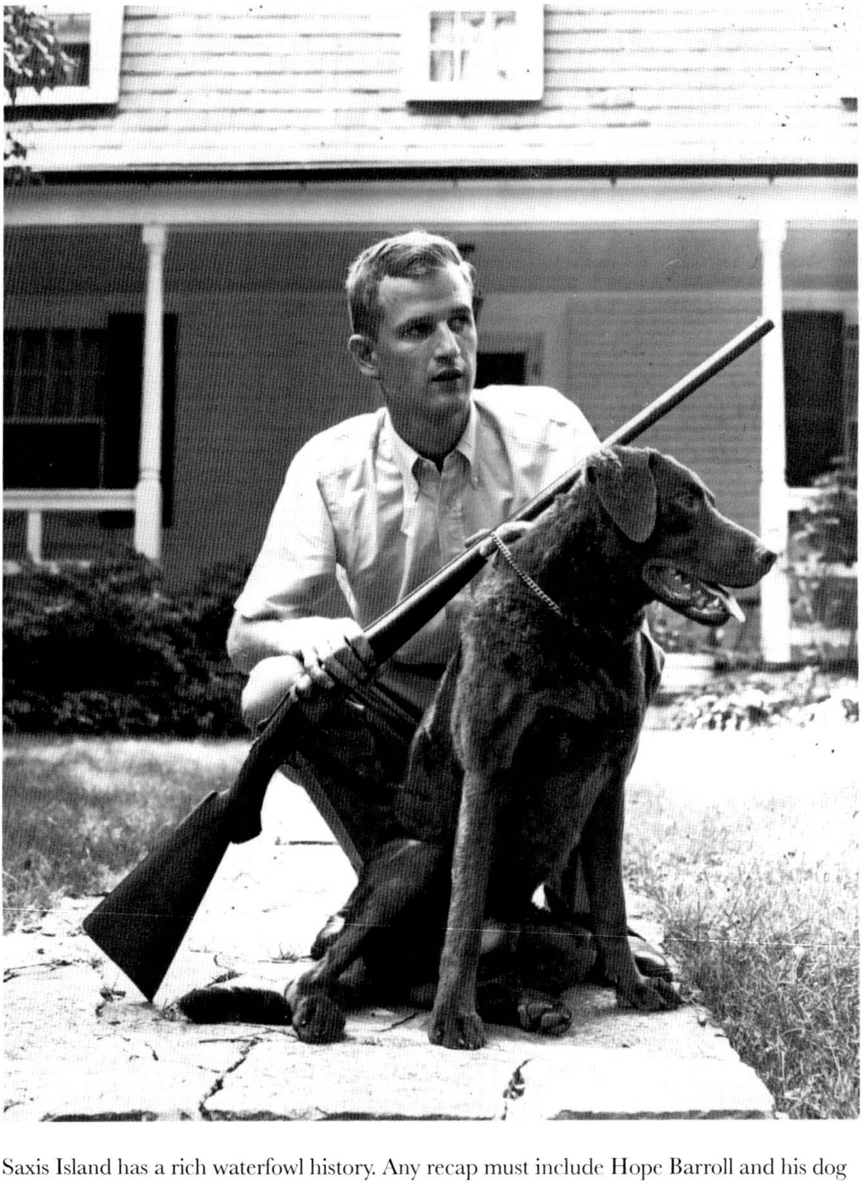

Saxis Island has a rich waterfowl history. Any recap must include Hope Barroll and his dog Gilly. *Saxis Island Museum.*

The labor involved in brushing the box blinds is becoming increasingly welcome as age creeps up on this old hunter. Cutting cedars and pines and selecting proper placement is a communal event. The usual suspects share the same passion and drive toward this endeavor. Getting them all in one place at the same time is quite an achievement. But as the work is being completed on a given weekend, it is evident that hope for a strong season burns in each of us. This optimism is tempered by the known fact that many things will go wrong. A few—very few—things will go as planned. Many more hours will be spent searching, prospecting and preparing than actually killing. Young hunters find this to be one of the hardest things to understand.

The joy of the sport is not found just in success. At some stages, greater satisfaction comes through the process. Boat rides in the darkness, the satisfaction of a good decoy placement, witnessing the infinite variety of sunrises and the wait for legal shooting all are part of the allure of the game. The simple joy of getting a bowl of hot soup on a cold morning, watching bald eagles hunting for their breakfast and witnessing the wildfowl that have no interest in our meager spread bring intrinsic satisfaction. Simply bearing witness to the wonders of nature is reason enough to go. The joy is in just being outside in the wild. These experiences will never fill the freezer, but sometimes, that's all we get. Often, it's enough.

As the end of the season nears, one of two scenarios will play out. If there are ducks around, there is a sense of urgency to pull in as many hunts as possible. If things are slow, the time between trips tends to get longer and longer. The 2015 season was dismal. It was undoubtedly the most disappointing season of my hunting career. This, combined with the fact that I wouldn't be able to hunt over the last weekend of the season, prompted this ill-advised trip on my last available day. It began as a culmination of all things that could go wrong actually going wrong. The northwest wind gusted at thirty miles an hour on a full-moon flood tide. Heading out of the harbor would be unwise. I elected to cut through Fishing Creek, which would leave only a two-hundred-yard stretch of the trip where I'd be exposed to the full extent of the Pocomoke Sound's fury. From there, I'd run sheltered up in the marsh, where I'd experienced a good teal shoot just three days prior.

Stepping out of the truck, I faced the full force of the wind. Spray was frothing white across the parking lot at Starlings Creek as the waves crashed headlong into the bulkhead. It was nautical. Walking back toward the boat to put the plug in, I noticed that the pop-up blind had come unhooked from its stanchion. The wind, or just the process of towing the boat, had pushed one side over with such force that it broke one of the bolts holding the stern section fast. I ran an electrical tie through it for a quick fix. The leg zipper on my bibs then broke, leaving three feet of Gore-Tex fabric flapping freely in the wind like the flag overlooking the Hurricane Grill. The tab on the chest zipper pulled off as well. Using a pair of needle-nosed pliers, I pulled the zipper up under my chin. Things were not going well. I was going to get wet.

As the sun was descending quickly in the western sky, I had the boat speeding across the basin and into the calm waters of Fishing Creek. Turning to the north, the chop picked up and increased in intensity as my chocolate lab Milo and I made our way closer to the sound. She was already lying on the floor as we faced the first few waves in the sound. Slowing somewhat and retracting from my usual standing position, it didn't take me long to realize that this was a very bad choice. The sixteen-foot aluminum boat was no match for the solid three- to four-footers on my bow. I quickly made the decision to turn around. Finding a lull in the rollers, I tried to make the turn as fast as possible. Though the boat was only broadside for a split second, a swell picked it up and rolled it on its chine. I was certain that it was going to flip, but I turned the motor hard to port. The boat somehow righted itself, and we averted disaster. The next wave broke across the transom, but soon we were back inside the shelter of the creek. Milo sensed the seriousness of the moment and took refuge on the middle seat.

Slowing the boat to pump it out, calm myself and check my gear, I decided to tie a small rig at Piney Hammocks. With the tide up, it would be a fine place to finish the season, and there were a few ducks using there. With only an hour to hunt, I hastily tossed out eight Herter's black duck decoys, hid the boat and got ready for action.

Now somewhat calm, I poured a cup of coffee. As I relaxed watching the buffleheads come and go, the fact that this was the last hunt of the season weighed heavy on my mind. The end of another season had arrived. Though we had not killed as many birds compared to other seasons, it was very satisfactory on many other levels. As the years have passed, I've learned that not every season should be judged by what's on the tally sheet. I replaced the tally sheet with a logbook long ago to provide insight into the reasons that each trip was memorable. This year's entries were dominated by the performance of our new chocolate lab, Milo, and the continued growth of my youngest son as a hunter.

As the list of "what ifs" began to creep into my mind, I was woken from my trance by Milo's change of posture. It's a scene I'd witnessed before. Her eyes gave away the position of the incoming birds. I reached for the old 1187 as the two mallards dropped in from over my right shoulder, quickly turned into the stiff northwest wind and hovered over the decoys. As the drake fell dead, the hen had already lit. My second shot missed low, but the third closed the deal. Milo, as usual, was off with the first shot. Her second retrieve was a bit long as the wind pushed the floating hen well offshore. Since it would be the last fetch of the year, I relished the experience.

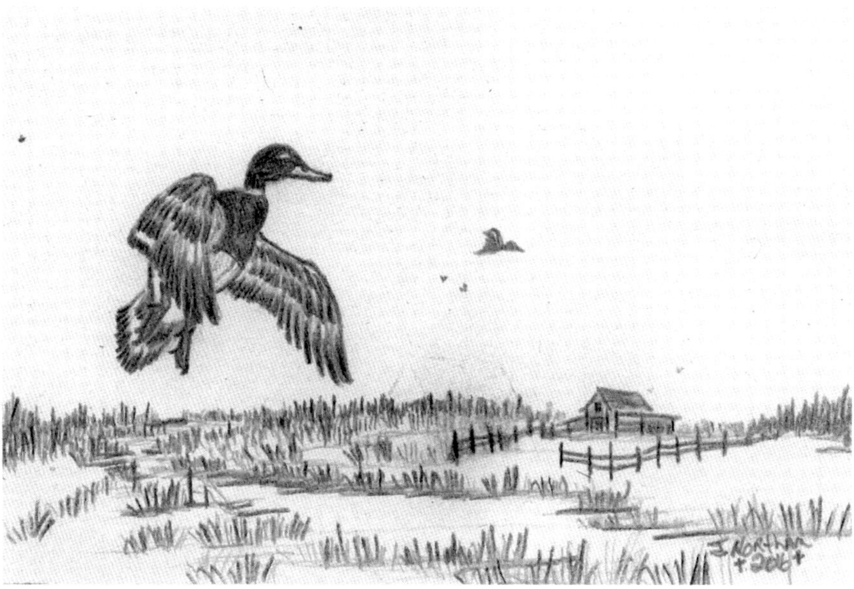

I didn't reload the gun. With Milo's return, the year was complete. She took her place on the bow, waiting for another chance. She knew she wouldn't get it when the gun was cased, signaling that her day was over. As she spent the next fifteen minutes picking up plastic bottles from the shoreline, I fell back into a reflective state on another season's end. Should I have spent more time scouting puddle ducks? Should I have hunted more on the seaside? Where were all the ducks? Why didn't I go to North Dakota this year? How will I stop the dog from breaking? How can I whack those divers rafted up off shore? I'll be pondering these questions over the next two hundred days.

More often than not, the season ends with us feeling unsatisfied. Most years end that way, as each season is compared inevitably to our best years. The desire to have a better year next year often overwhelms us at season's end. Realizing that our successes are a direct result of overcoming our numerous failures will serve as a confidence builder over the long offseason.

BERNARD ISLAND BEAT DOWN

In the early to mid-1980s, we ran hunting parties for extra money. These funds aided in my survival of the spring semesters at Elon College. Much of it was spent on beer, women, whiskey and food. The rest of it was simply wasted.

This day's trip was for an auctioneer from upper Delaware and some of his friends. I'd booked the trip as the result of a referral. Standing in the living room, I heard an approaching vehicle and watched as this fella turned into what he thought was the driveway. In actuality, it was the junction of Accomack County Road 695 and Jacks Creek. I watched his headlights rise to the sky as he crossed the curb and then plummet three feet directly down in the soft mud. The whole front of his Suburban was immersed in ditchwater. Like rats from a sinking ship, the four men scurried out to the blacktop to survey the situation. No one was hurt, and in a few minutes, one of my buddies showed up with a truck with enough strength to pull him out.

None the worse, we headed for the ramp at Hammocks, where the scow was waiting. While loading the gear, I noticed that the northwest wind was much stronger than the ten miles per hour the weathermen were calling for. These folks wanted to shoot divers, and I knew where a few should be. We headed for a small island just outside Cattail Creek where I had a box blind with a boat hide. After unloading the gear and the sports, I quickly set the diver decoys and then ran one hundred or so yards out toward Cattail Channel, pulled up the bait stake and moved it to a spot about thirty-five yards from the left side of the blind. This placement would provide excellent decoying shots.

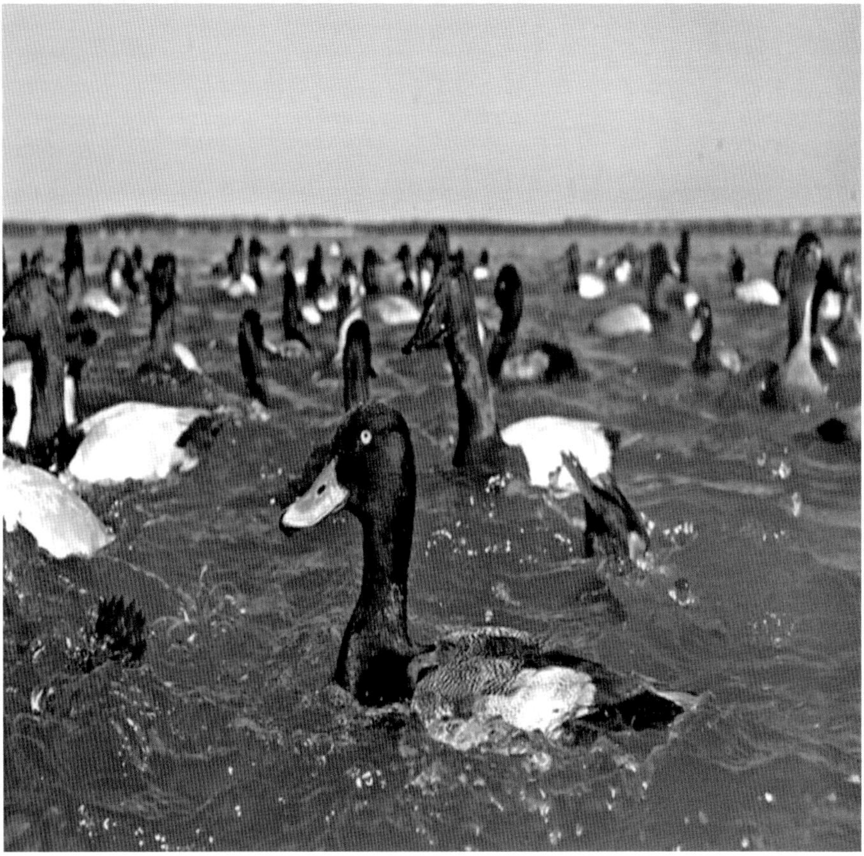

Raft ducks, like canvasbacks and bluebills, tend to lose their natural wariness when exposed to corn and become fairly predictable. They can be conditioned to follow the bait stake wherever it happens to move. *Paul Bramble photo.*

We'd used this bait stake method successfully for a while. The birds would key on the stake, knowing that there would be food around it. They come to the stake without hesitation. While I was out of town the previous week, my father had hunted this blind. He and his partner shot their twenty bluebills, moved the stake back off shore and left rather quickly. It was a hotspot in more ways than one.

These folks were seasoned hunters. They did not need me sitting in the blind calling their shots. They knew how the game was played and were good at it. Shooting began immediately as I pulled the boat in the skiff blind. Butler, my Chesapeake, went from chilling in the boat to being fully engaged very quickly. That would be the theme of the day.

The wind continued to pick up. As the tide rose, the waves began to lap at the windward side of the blind. I monitored this from my vantage point in the boat as they continued to grind on the divers. I knew the auctioneer fella pretty well, but it was my first encounter with the other three. One stood out as an exceptional shot. As the wind and waves increased, I noticed him consistently pull two or more birds out of each flock. He apparently was among the nation's best trap shooters. He was living up to his reputation on this day.

The waves now covered the island, and it was clear to me that we had to pull out. I walked to the blind to discuss a plan with the party. I explained the situation and gave them a few options. We opted to run from our location to Lower Bernard Island.

The run would be wet but not too bad, as the waves would be on our starboard until we made the leeward side of the island. Making our turn into the wind, I could see that the wind had continued to increase, now blowing a constant twenty-five miles per hour. With the tide up, hundreds of bluebills, cans and redheads rose from the shelter of the island as we closed in on it. I tied a rig of about two dozen tightly packed divers. Concealed from the birds in our brush blind, I realized that this was going to be one to remember. The first flock I saw was a bunch of eight tiptoeing across the water directly into the northwest wind and coming straight for us. There was no circling or indecision. All eight lay belly up in the decoys. Butler did the best he could, but we were downing them quicker and in larger numbers than he could handle. I'd venture out in the boat every fifteen minutes or so to pick up dead birds and find what few cripples I could see. The salvo continued for about two hours.

Cold, wet from the spray crossing the island and running low on ammo, we decided to pull out. Ice had formed on everything that had gotten wet. I beat what I could off the decoys, but admittedly, it was a poor job. Loaded with four men, a Chesapeake, gear and me, the twenty-foot scow was right at capacity. The added weight of the ice and several sack bags of birds pushed it to its limit. Just on plane, I rounded the sandbar on the east end of the island. The first three waves rolled across the bow into the boat. Travel back to our launching point, Hammocks, would be unsafe. I made the decision to sail fair wind into Guard Shore. It would be a pain dealing with all that the decision would entail, but at least we would arrive alive. The same outcome would be uncertain with any other choice. My guests seemed thankful to step off the boat at Guard Shore. I was as well.

I instructed them to hide the five bags of ducks out of sight in the rocks around the ramp. In search of a phone, I began the long, cold walk up the road to the nearest house. Thankfully, a sightseer came along and gave me a ride back to Sanford to retrieve my truck, trailer and some hot soup for my party. Upon my return, they gave me a deposit for the following Saturday.

As we rode back in the truck, it was obvious that this group had a very memorable hunting experience, one that they would recount time and time again in passing years. It was a full hunt with elements of danger, foul weather, lots of birds, incredible shooting and an uncertain outcome.

I was fortunate to be part of it.

BERTHA

Just inside the sandbar on the end of Upper Bernard Island, the black duck seemed to know that we were hunkered down in the blind. It also thought that it was safe at distance of about seventy yards. This would be Bertha's first test.

Shouldering the fifteen-pound beast slowly, I took aim about four inches above the swimming ducks head. After I squeezed the trigger, the bird appeared to "jump" into the pattern. Lifting just off the water, the Federal No. 4 lead stopped his ascent. It became clear at that moment that the investment would pay off.

"Bertha," as we called the gun, was a ten-gauge Ithaca automatic. It shot a three-and-a-half-inch shell in the days when many were still using two-and-three-quarter-inch loads. It was like nothing I had ever seen before. On a trip to Chestertown back in 1977, we shared a pit with a gentleman from Rocky Mount, North Carolina. We were amazed at the swath he could cut through decoying geese. We were even more shocked at the distances at which he could cleanly drop a goose. In that pit, on that cold November morning, we vowed to own one before the coming weekend. Sure enough we found one in Jaxon's Hardware just fifteen minutes from our house in Sanford. This proved the old adage that if Jaxon's doesn't have it, you probably don't need it.

We primarily bought the gun just for those black ducks that would always seem to hang up outside the decoys, often at a range of about seventy yards. In those days, the ten gauge was the only option for this distance, and it earned its keep time and time again. Equipped with an extra-full choke and thirty-four-inch barrel, its pattern was about the size

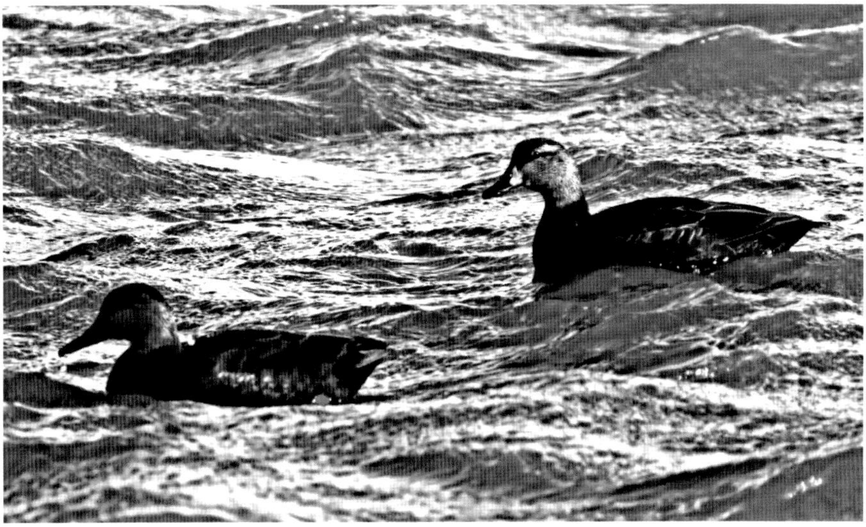

Our addition of Bertha, a ten-gauge automatic equipped with an extra-full choke, was absolutely deadly on black ducks that were hung up outside of the decoys. *Paul Bramble photo.*

of a large pizza at fifty yards. At seventy, it wasn't much larger. It was a long-range killing machine.

This claim was substantiated on a windless Saturday morning in a stilted box blind near Tolchester Marina. Six of us sat abreast, hovered over a spread of a dozen sets of V-boards in hopes of pulling down our limit of a Canada goose apiece. I was positioned on the far left of the blind, next to the door, and handled the calling and retrieving chores for the day. Things had been slow that morning. Our group had a single early in the morning, and then about nine o'clock, we coaxed a pair from an adjacent hunter into our decoys. The two had little chance of escape. As the day wore on it, was clear that lunch might be the highlight of the trip. We decided to pull out at eleven. Just as we were about to start packing up, a single goose made his way from the bay toward the decoys. Being a bluebird day, and with all the movement inside the blind as we prepared for our departure, there was little chance that this bird was going to surrender to the decoys. If there was to be a shot had, it would be a long, passing shot.

We spied the single invader at a distance of one hundred yards. Flying at a height of sixty yards above the water, the goose didn't change the frequency of its wing beats. The gunner at the far right of the blind was the first to fire. As the goose came to a distance of fifty yards and rising, this hunter's effort yielded no results. Right down the line, the same scenario played out.

When the hunter to my right had exhausted his efforts, I raised Bertha. At a distance of sixty-five yards and fleeing fast, the goose looked to be home free. A single shot with adequate lead sent the bird tumbling to the water below. Five men peered left in unison, wondering what cannon I was shooting. I'd seen that look before. I'm quite sure that another ten mag was sold right then and there.

With the banning of lead shot, I had to make some alterations to the gun. Steel wouldn't pattern the same at distance and lacked the killing energy. I decided to cut the barrel down and rechoke to an improved cylinder. Plus, after we cut the barrel down to a manageable thirty inches, the gun became a more nimble weapon. Though its distance killing prowess would be compromised, it could now cut though a flock of incoming fowl.

On a cold, snowy, windblown Saturday morning, Bill Hall and I crawled through a thin strip of pine forest that bordered a winter wheat field. The cold conditions had a flock of about five hundred snow geese feeding in tight proximity to one another. The high winds had them in the shelter of the pines. Things were ripe for the picking. Approaching through the woods, we had the wind in our favor. Hidden thorn bushes pushed down by the snow and a small creek that we were unaware of obstructed our crawl toward the geese. Staying low and working slow, we made our way closer and closer to the geese. Rising along a fallen pine tree just ten yards inside the wood line, we peered above the fallen timber at the mass of gurgling geese. They fed greedily, unaware of our presence, just thirty yards from us.

Withdrawing to a position behind the fallen tree, we agreed that we'd rise, shoulder our guns and wait until we had a nice "wad" of geese knotted up. The signal would be given, and we'd unleash hell on them. Slowly coming to our knees, we sought solid rest for our guns as we waited for the right time. I nodded to my partner, and we slapped the tree trunk to get their heads and necks up in a more venerable position. The countdown from three began. Bertha, braced by my left hand and the trunk of the fallen tree, was directed at the thickest mass of fowl. Our guns spoke first in unison, then in rhythmic timing. We each got off two shots while they were still on the ground and our third as they were getting airborne. On the third, the path Bertha cut was incredible. Picking out the single goose closest to me, I pulled the trigger, and geese from the shot funnel fell dead from thirty to sixty yards. Fourteen shots later, all of the cripples were dispatched. Thirty-seven snows were loaded into the back of the F-100, and we were off looking to do it again. There's nothing quite like a good ground swat.

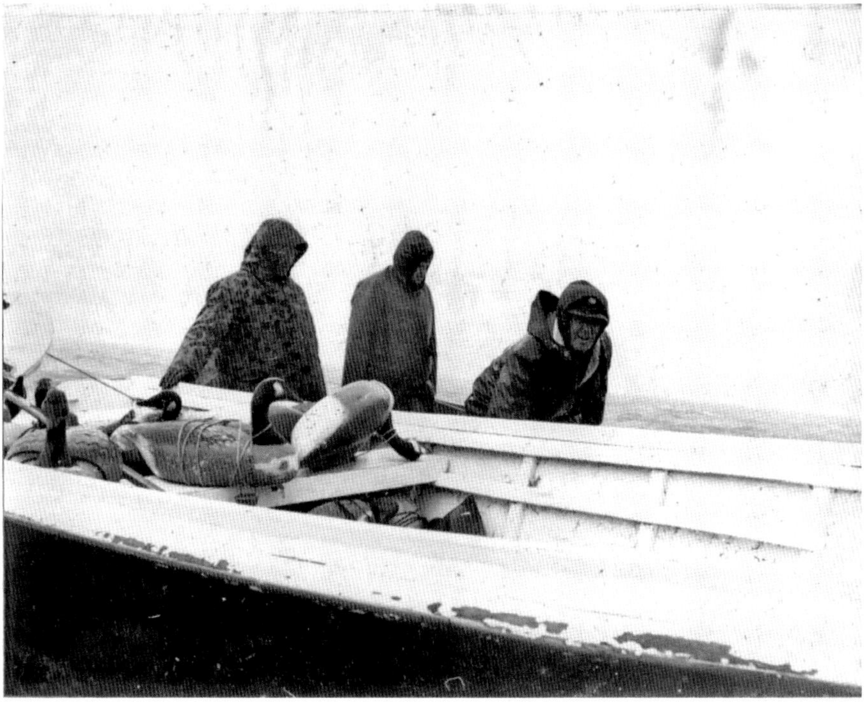

Bunk Evans (right) and his goose-hunting party wade the scow along the sandy bottom of Drum Bay while picking up decoys. *Saxis Island Museum.*

With the advent of the three-and-a-half-inch twelve gauge and the prohibitive cost of ammo for it, I relegated Bertha to a place far back in the gun safe. These days, I take it out only for semiannual cleaning and the occasional turkey hunt. I don't care if I ever shoot that gun again; just holding it brings back a cavalcade of memories worth many times more than the value of the gun.

BLUEBILLS BROKE LOOSE

The bluebills had finally arrived in Saxis. All the prognosticators had pointed to a record population of these speedy divers, and we'd patiently awaited our whack at 'em. We'd done our due diligence and knew with the coming northwest wind where they would likely be heading for shelter. All there was to do now was execute properly.

My decoy rig was able, and it had been seasoned by those who had come before me. Lou Spence, arguably the best wing shot to come off Saxis, had given them to my uncle who had passed them to me. The two dozen inflatable Victor blackheads showed the wear of countless days bobbing in the waters off Great Fox Island. They had developed their character by bouncing in the bottom of Lou's skiff on the way to the Saxis Island Gun Club. A few were strafed by gunfire and had been patched with 5200 marine sealant, which had been properly painted over. Though not overly large, their high profile made them a fine gunning stool. I'd used them a bit, and as I loaded them in the boat, thoughts of decoying flocks of bluebills ran though my head again and again. I'd waited for this a long time.

My father had recently taken up decoy carving in preparation for his pending retirement. He worked hard to develop a gunning rig style of his own. His brother Danny had picked it up much earlier and had a style that made it look easy. He's a natural. He'd polished his skills with the Ward brothers, and his body style and paint schemes greatly resembled theirs. Dad had to work at it, but he found his groove and began to steadily produce pieces of increasing quality. He'd been working on a diver body pattern for

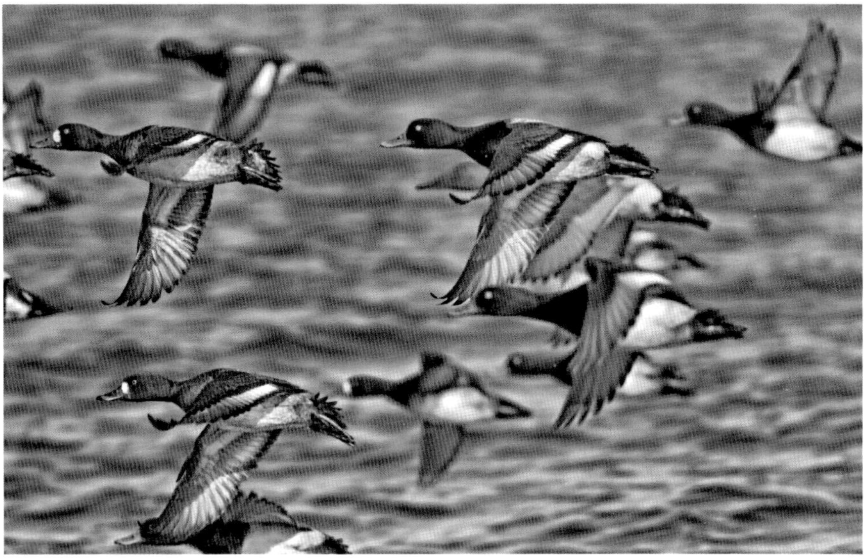

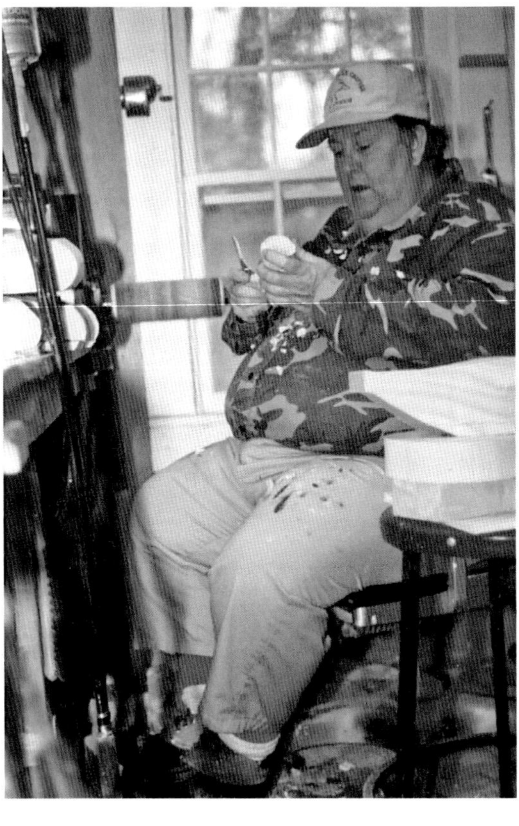

Above: Often decoying in large flocks, bluebill hunting can be a truly memorable experience. Practice and patience are required to know when to call the shot. *Paul Bramble photo.*

Left: Nothing rides the water like a handmade decoy. From his shop in Sanford, Virginia, Carroll Lee Marshall can be found carving them out daily. His working-style decoys are a favorite among hunters and collectors alike. *Paul Bramble photo.*

the last month and found one he liked. He'd finished a pair that I thought were representative of Saxis Island hunting decoys.

Sleep didn't come easy in anticipation of the coming events. It seemed I woke every thirty minutes and checked the alarm. Finally, forty minutes before the alarm was set to go off, I couldn't take it anymore. I got up, made coffee, packed a breakfast snack and began to make my way down to pick up Dad. The fog was somewhat thick, so it took a little longer than usual to reach his house. I was glad I had gotten up early because I'd burned my extra time in travel. He, too, was quite excited, up and ready to go. We quickly loaded his gun and shells, and he set a burlap sack atop my stack of diver decoys. I didn't think much of it.

The run to our Deep Hole gut blind is an easy go. Less than two miles from the dock, we followed the shoreline closely in the dense fog. It took longer than normal, but shortly, we were at our blind. We unloaded our gear at the blind, and with legal shooting coming in ten minutes, I was about to begin the task of setting the decoys. He motioned for me to wait, so I did. From the burlap sack, he produced two hand-carved bluebills with keels, properly weighted, rigged and ready to go. They were the prettiest gunning stools I'd ever hunted over. I carefully placed them on the stern seat and got to my task.

We like to deploy our divers with a power alley, aka landing zone, right in front of the blind. The birds were just starting to fly as I positioned his two hand-carved beauties upwind on the outside. With the rig to my satisfaction, I idled the skiff up the creek to its hiding place. As I cinched the half hitch on the mooring stob, Dad waxed a single. Butler scooped it up nicely. I quickly made my way to the blind. Surveying the rig, I was satisfied with the way things were looking. On the upwind side, I noticed that Dad's hand-carved pair had broken loose and was drifting away freely with aid of the outgoing tide and stiffening northwest wind. Apparently the small nail, or brad, that he had used as a fastener on a leather loop had given way. *Shit*, I thought. I had to retrieve them.

With haste I made my way back to the skiff to make the retrieve. As I cranked the engine, he shot again. Twice. Not wanting to throw a wake through the decoys, I trolled upwind past the spread and jumped the boat on plane to find the drifting dekes in the lifting fog. Three more shots rang out, and I was missing it.

Finally, I found the decoys, securely reattached a suitable decoy cord and weight and reset them in the spread. As I entered the creek just north of the blind, my dad's Browning spoke three more times. As I stepped out of the

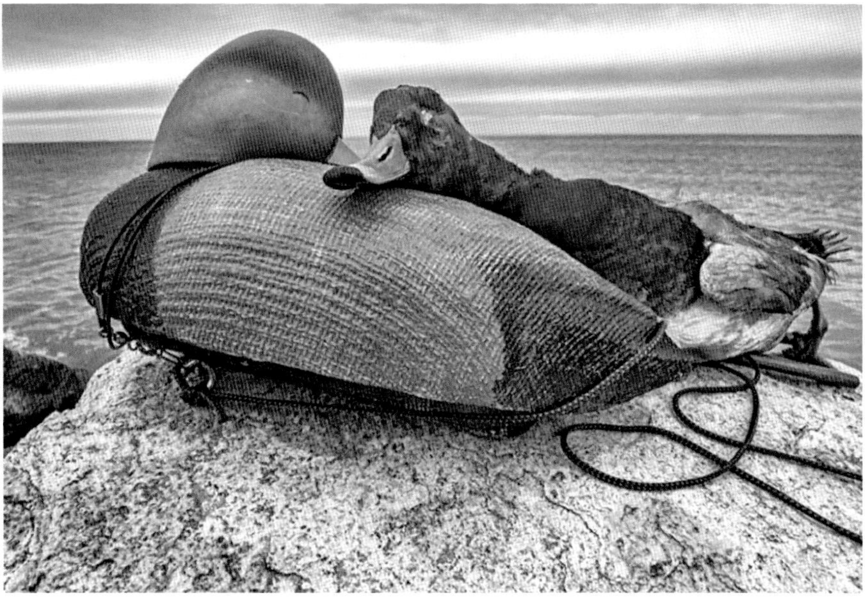

There's something uniquely satisfying about successfully hunting over handmade decoys. They ride better and last longer than their plastic rivals. *Paul Bramble photo.*

boat, he shot twice more. Finally, I got in the blind. His gun was cased. In about twenty minutes, he'd killed his limit of ten bluebills, and I'd not yet uncased my gun. Though happy for his success, I admit that I was more than a little steamed.

"I've waited all year for this, and I'm not gonna get in on it!" jumped from my mouth as I quickly loaded my gun. But the flight of birds continued. He just sat there, sipped coffee and heckled me until I'd got my ten. That didn't take long on this day.

CATTAIL CREEK OUTLAWS

For forty years, the Marshall family has hunted the same tump of land near Cattail Creek. With very few exceptions, we can be found there each and every Thanksgiving morning. We've always maintained some sort of box blind in this creek, and it has been the setting for many memories. Such was the case on November 23, 1978.

On this Thanksgiving morning, our party of five included my father, my grandfather Marvin G. White, my gunning partner Bill Hall and his father. Neither Marvin nor Bill Hall Sr. had been waterfowl hunting in twenty years. We were elated to have them join my father and I on this overcast Thanksgiving morning. The elders hunted in the box blind on the island while Bill and I elected for a skiff blind on the next point up the creek. Our scouting hadn't provided much to get excited about, but it was Thanksgiving; our plan was to relax and enjoy the day.

We'd been up the creek no more than three times since the water cooled sufficiently to move the rockfish out of the creek. Two trips were made to create the skiff blind that Bill and I occupied. The other trip was to bush the box blind on the island and spiffy up the boat hide. We hadn't encountered any major storms over the year, so our stuff was left relatively intact. Occasionally that fall, we'd set our small net off Cattail Point, where we caught perch and rockfish. During these trips, we observed several flocks of geese that were using the area but very few ducks. Our expectation on that day was to have very few visitors.

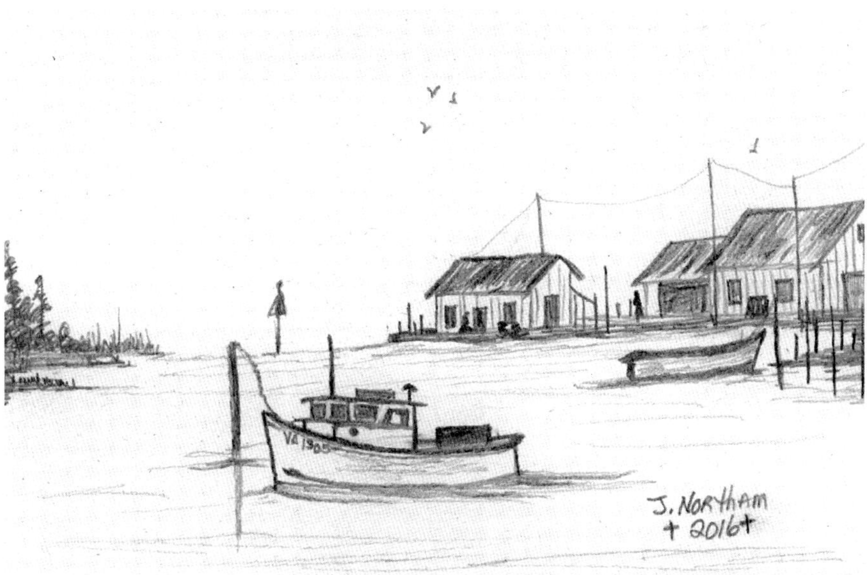

Our morning started with grilled ham-and-egg sandwiches at my father's carving shop in Sanford. We filled our Stanleys with hot coffee and made our way to the ramp. On the rising tide, we five hunters sailed easily through Rock Gut and across Cattail Channel. It was an uneventful trip that I'd made many times. I came off the throttle as we reached the mouth of Cattail Creek. With the light northwest wind on my stern, I began to formulate a plan for decoy placement once the blind came into view in the predawn glow. Marvin and Billy appeared to be having a very good time. As they stepped out of the scow onto the soft soil of the island, they were talking about the last time they went hunting. Both trips ended badly.

After unloading our gear and the three hunters, Bill and I set about tying their rig. I tied a few bufflehead decoys on the side of the island, fifteen geese in front of the blind and a dozen or so black ducks inside the geese and a bit downwind. It was a small spread, but it looked pretty natural. Quickly we made our way up the creek to our skiff blind and set a very similar spread. With five minutes to legal, we pulled in the blind. Our guns were promptly loaded, and I poured cups of coffee as we watched the time closely. Finishing my cup, I watched as a single bufflehead made its way through the gauntlet down the creek from us. He buzzed our decoys at a distance of thirty-five yards. The Federal No. 4 stopped him dead.

The bird hadn't finished kicking when I heard the outboard engine crank up less than a mile from us. The timing was a bit odd, and the location was equally baffling. But we had birds to kill and hadn't anything to worry about—or so we thought.

I could see the boat coming. It was an olive drab eighteen-foot scow much like mine. This one sported a 150-horsepower Mercury. I knew who it was instantly. It was Bill Richardson, a game warden whom I'd heard about but never formally met. The other times I'd been checked by the law, they generally waited until eight o'clock or so. Never had they come so hastily just after legal shooting time had passed. This time, they came with urgency.

Their boat didn't come off plane as they passed Dad and his group of hunters in the box. Just outside our decoys, they throttled back. The boat settled as the swell created by the sudden deceleration pushed ahead, making our boat roll severely. Coming alongside, they asked that we unload our guns and join them over on the island. They said it would make the check go much easier. So Bill and I did as they asked. Once on the island, the process began. It seemed fairly routine at first, but quickly we could see that things had taken a turn for the worse.

They were here to write us tickets for shooting over bait, a charge for which we were certainly innocent. The two officers explained that they had been to the blinds within the week and had found corn placed directly in front of each of the blinds. I was certain that no one in our party had put it there. I was also fairly certain who had. We'd had a run-in with a fellow up there the year prior. Thinking he had clearly gotten the message that he was not welcome up that creek, we felt that the issue had been put to bed. He would have to atone for his actions or face the consequences. Since he wouldn't fess up to his actions, he settled for the latter. He didn't know of the severity or the hour of our reply. It was a costly mistake on his part.

The wardens went through the whole nine yards. They checked life jackets, registrations, safety equipment and everything down the line. Though we protested vociferously on our innocence to this charge, they wrote the tickets anyway. That had been decided earlier in the week. With the fines relatively minimal for such an offence back then, it was much easier to pay the fine than hire a lawyer and be off to court for the day. Since I was under the age of sixteen, I was the only one exempt. The process started with my father. The warden asked a few questions, trying to trip him up during the write up, but he held fast.

My grandfather was a wreck. He was pacing and obviously nervous. He handed the warden his license, and his turn began. Looking through the pile of licenses the warden had collected, Richardson asked my grandfather for his name.

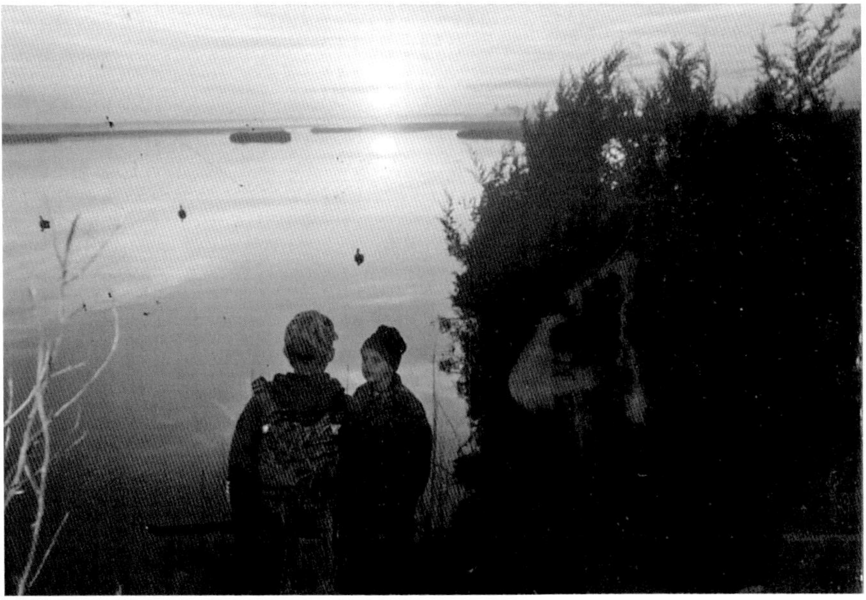

Standing in front of the same blind that our family has hunted continually for over forty years, my two boys discussed the morning's events. I wonder what they were saying. *C.L. Marshall photo.*

"M.G. White," he replied.

"What's the M.G. stand for?"

"Marvin."

It was then that the gravity of the situation struck my grandfather. He was going to get a ticket.

"What's the G stand for?" Richardson asked.

Marvin replied, "Oh God!"

We four burst out laughing, and the wardens chuckled a bit also. Billy told him that he doubted Royal, his father, had used that for his middle name.

The years passed, and my grandfather occasionally hunted with my cousin. He grew to enjoy it more as a social activity than anything else. Billy Hall Sr. didn't duck hunt again but spent his time afield chasing quail.

After my grandfather's passing, I was participating in the unenviable task of going through his belongings. Folks of his generation placed valuable information in the family Bible. Going through his, I found his ticket, summons and $100 canceled check for his game violation.

It made me smile.

DEDICATION TO THE CAUSE

It had been a good season thus far. Teal had been plentiful, and we were on them. We'd had several good hunts in a row, and with forecast of the wind moving from the southeast to the northwest in the morning at near gale force, we were poised to pounce on them again.

Such wind is not conducive for my sixteen-foot aluminum skiff. We opted to run Donnie Porter's eighteen-foot fiberglass Manatee to our favorite teal spot, the Spank Box. The Spank Box requires a half-hour run crossing the open waters of Messongo Creek and then up the sheltered tributary for six or so miles. It's a fairly safe run, but one that must be undertaken in the darkness if you're going to be successful on this teal hunt. They come early up there, and it's a very fast and furious shoot.

I met Donnie at the appointed time at our little hunting retreat in Sanford. We were a little ahead of schedule, so after the gear was loaded in the Manatee, we opted for a cup of coffee before we headed to the ramp. Since we were still a little bleary-eyed from the night before, the coffee was welcomed. As we sat and sipped the coffee, Donnie observed that the wind had yet to turn. Thinking nothing of it, we finished our cups and headed off to the truck.

We were welcomed by a spitting rain as we wheeled around in the parking lot at Hammocks and positioned the boat at the throat of the ramp. There, final checks were made, gear checked and raincoats donned. Wind from the southeast blows directly in the ramp at Hammocks. The waves were nearly white capping in the area where we were about to launch the

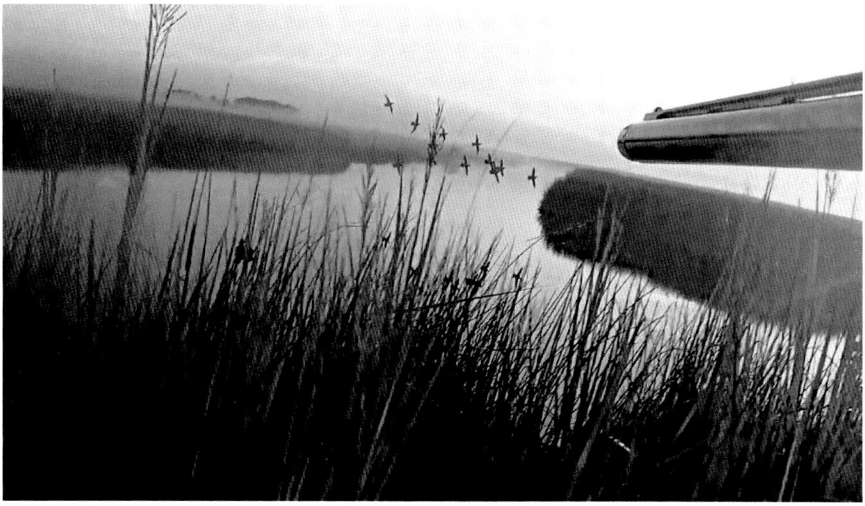

Teal can provide fast and furious action. These tasty little targets fly early and often in tight bunches. *Paul Bramble photo.*

boat. Launching the boat would have to be a quick production. To achieve this, Donnie got in the boat, and I backed it down the ramp where it floated off. He started the motor as I pulled the truck out of the ramp. The plan was for Donnie to launch the boat and spin it around, bow to the seas, while waiting for me and my golden retriever to return. It seemed like a good plan.

By the time I got back down to the ramp, it was evident that all had not gone well. The dog had sprinted to the boat and jumped in. The engine had stalled in the frothy seas, and by the time he got it going again, it was full of water. It happened quickly, and there was no time for me to lend aid. When the boat went beam sea, another broke in it. The half-full gas tank was floating along the gunnel, and Donnie did the only thing he could do: he got the boat bow in seas and punched it. Water, decoys, gear and a golden retriever washed astern as the Yamaha 85 tried desperately to rise to plane. It just didn't have enough horsepower to push the load.

Trying to rid the hull of water, the boat was moving away from the dock at a slow but steady rate. The engine was straining from the enormous weight in the hull. From my vantage point on the dock, it was evident that most likely this was going to be a very serious problem with the high probability of losing the entire mess. But Donnie is more than a little salty.

To the east of the launch ramp is a loading pier, and just up the creek from that is an old railway. Most folks who launch at Hammocks have seen it but most likely never paid any attention to it. He survived the turn to port, missed the loading pier and, with the swells on his stern, rode that Manatee up the railway as far as it would go. We grabbed the guns and what gear we could and tossed them out on dry land, watching as waves continued to pound the stern of the skiff. The dog was confused as hell. Quickly, we unhitched the trailer, backed the truck to the head of the railway, attached the bow line to the trailer ball and pulled it up on the rail and out of harm's way. We hopped aboard with five-gallon buckets and bailed it dry. At this point, we'd survived imminent danger, the boat was still in one piece, the gear was salvaged and all was in good shape. Plus, we still had forty minutes until legal shooting time.

Most would have packed it in. But we had forty minutes, and we knew that the ducks would be coming. We removed the motor's cover, gave it a good dousing of WD-40 and commenced to reload the boat. Fortunately, Leonard White's crab house provided a bit of shelter from the wind, which enabled us to slide the boat off the rails, get it running and head to the Spank Box. Getting the boat out on plane, I pulled the drain plug and safely stowed it in my zippered chest pocket. It wasn't long before we made the lee side of Green Point. Things got much better from there. Quickly, the boat drained, and I replaced the plug. It would have been easy to toss in the towel, just head on over to Martha's Kitchen for hot coffee and a Graveyard Dead

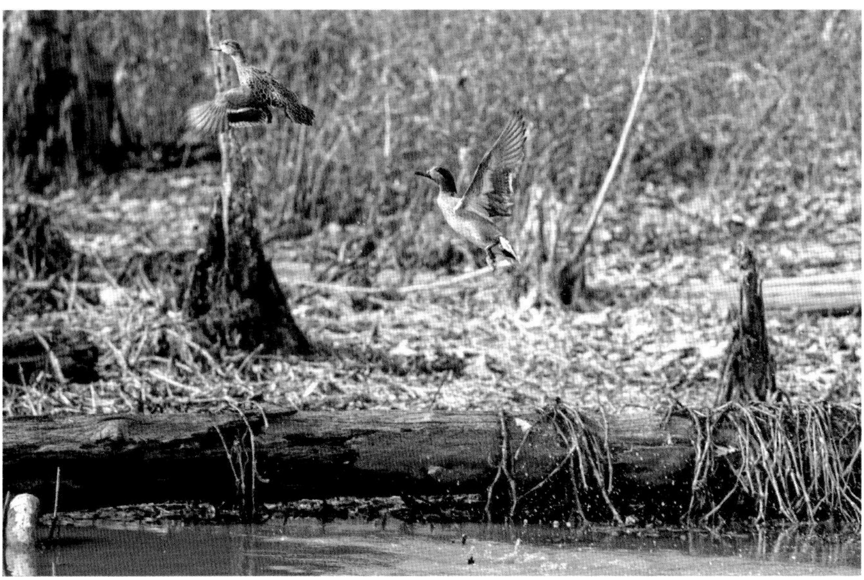

Brackish water marshes are a favorite haunt of greenwing teal. Quick shooting is a must to achieve a full bag. *Paul Bramble photo.*

breakfast special. But there were ducks out there for us to get, and we damn sure were going do our part to get them.

The teal flew low, and we shot well. One hour later, we were picking up decoys with two limits of teal lying on the bow. It was an especially satisfying hunt in light of the troubles we'd had in getting there. We weren't sure how many other folks would have had such dedication to the cause, but we were damn sure glad that we did. I had a little grin on my face all day at work.

DUCK HUNTING VALHALLA

Robert Ruark, in *The Old Man and the Boy*, wrote, "The old man used to say the best part of hunting and fishing was the thinking about going and the talking about it after you got back." Most boys wouldn't understand that quote. For many younger hunters of the *Duck Dynasty* age, it's about shooting and the lifestyle. As I get older, it has become more about the thinking and talking than the trigger pulling.

This addiction started innocently enough. I begged my father to let me tag along with him and old Walton Taylor on the occasional hunt up on "the mud." It is an area near the mouth of the Pocomoke River where he and Walton had made an offshore blind. Walton was more than a little cynical when it came to cover and motion. He made certain that our faces were pressed to the floor and chastised us for even thinking about looking up to prevent flaring decoying fowl. Often Walton would be the only one to get a shot off. He saved the life of many a goose with his off-key voice calling. I vividly remember the utter demoralized look on his face after he whiffed on a pair of canvasbacks. To him, it was more than a hobby; it was a way of life. He took it seriously, and I liked it.

It always seemed like something that I should do. It came naturally. It didn't seem like work. Early on, I learned that there were many things appealing to me about this duck hunting thing. It's a very fluid endeavor requiring thought, planning and execution. But no two days are alike. Learning the skills to deal with the myriad issues that must be overcome to be consistently successful is critical.

The skills that make a person a good duck hunter are skills worth having. You must be motivated to play this game. You must be motivated to get out of bed at ungodly hours. You must stay motivated to keep the massive amount of gear in good working order. The tasks are unending. Over home, we called those who lacked the motivation to build adequate blinds and left their gear in disarray "stump gunners." That was not a label you wanted to get.

A good duck hunter is resourceful. Whether it is in building blinds, cutting cedars or gaining access to additional hunting opportunities, resourcefulness and self-reliance will yield rewards. Many times, hunters are faced with dire situations: a broken-down motor, a skiff left ashore by the falling tide or being forced to decide on the best and safest route back to the dock in the evening darkness. There is no room for indecision in instances like these. Self-reliance gained by conquering such difficulties adds to the character of a man. And these days, self-reliance, and the confidence that goes with it, is a dwindling commodity.

Weatherman. Mechanic. Fabricator. Captain. Farmer. Artist. Husband. Father. Teacher. These titles represent just a few of the skills that must, in some degree, be understood to be a waterfowl hunter. Develop an understanding of each of these, and satisfaction, to some degree, will follow. Fall short in any one of the aforementioned disciplines, and the outcome would be less than desirable. Sometimes it could be downright dangerous.

We're a heady bunch, spending most of our time thinking about this passion, and that often interferes with what non duck hunters think we should do with our time. Social events, especially those that call for late-night activity, are attended sporadically during hunting season. When such an event becomes a pressing matter, we seek kindred spirits and usually gather off to the side of the bar. Discussion topics range from brands of shells, how to patch waders, duck boats, dogs and who shot what. It's usually a tightknit group, a cult in and of itself. As non hunters stop to chat, we're cordial, but the minute they leave, we're right back immersed in ducks and all that goes with them. Those who don't hunt won't be able to be involved in the conversation. They wouldn't understand. They haven't earned the right.

Without regard for social standing, duck hunters judge and are judged, somewhat harshly, by their peers. Judgment is often not based on the number of birds in the bag. More often than not, it comes down to how the person is to hunt with, if they have a proper moral compass and their work ethic. Who but other hunters would put up with the stuff that we as hunters routinely endure? We consider leaky waders, nor'easter blown-out ebb tides, mud flats, broken push poles, trucks buried up to the axle, prop-wrapped decoy lines and cold coffee just part of what makes up a duck season. An inclusive fraternity with a lingo all our own, most of us are willing to teach yet reluctant to share.

Beginning usually in late September, coinciding with the arrival of the first migratory Canada geese, our gears shift from whatever else we were doing to waterfowl hunting. For ten months during the year, folks who are first to volunteer for civic duties begin to be hard to find. The husband who can't remember the five items on the grocery list is absolutely fastidious in the preparation of his blind bag. This sacred vestibule is stuffed full of all sorts of "necessities" that cannot be done without. Several times per year, it's reorganized, and after each trip, it's restocked. It's worse than a woman's purse.

Over time, it has become standard operating procedure that holidays, weekends, days off, available afternoons, most mornings and virtually any available time will be spent in some waterfowl-related endeavor. Scouting, blind building, decoy rigging and, if time allows, actually hunting become the normal excuses as we routinely miss dinner, meetings, ball games and the other things that make up a normal life. Once this hunting thing grabs you, any semblance of a normal life goes out the window for three months a year. It's understandable. The call of the marshes to the duck hunter is strong. It's

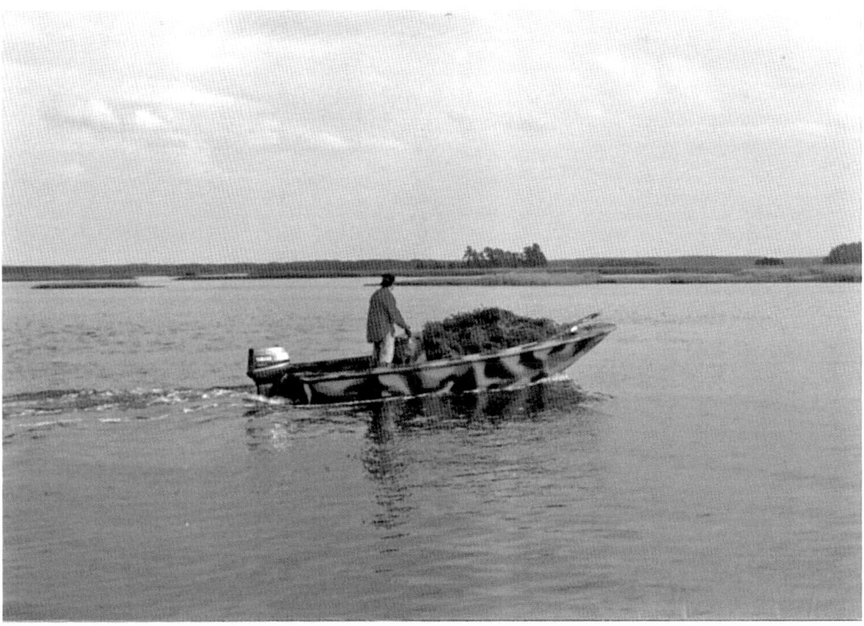

Duck season goes far beyond the allotted hunting days. Blind building and repair, scouting and bushing happen throughout the year. *Marlene Marshall photo.*

consuming. Attempts to change the duck hunter will remain futile, as they have since the beginning of time. My wife can certainly attest to that.

We've all shared that feeling. The ducks have arrived, the blinds are set and the decoys rigged and ready. The boat is tuned and full of fuel. The desire to stand on the soft soil of the saltmarsh, parting the brushes to peer across the wind-whipped water for what Mother Nature has to offer, is unquenchable. It's food for the soul. Some say it is soul food in the most natural form. The sight of spent gun shells floating on the outgoing tide is satisfying, like a salve applied to a bug bite. The smell of burnt gunpowder is aromatic. It dissipates quickly, but the short exposure is pleasurable, memorable and irreplaceable.

One of the greatest attributes of a duck hunter is the ability to deal with the seemingly endless frustration that occurs on a somewhat regular basis. Punished by forces that are beyond our control, such as weather, wind and tide, we vainly attempt to work these influences to our favor. More often than not, our efforts are to no avail. Reward is a rarity. But our hope and efforts are sometimes rewarded just enough through the experience or the shooting (or at times a combination of both) to make it all seem worthwhile. Such experiences are drawn on in lean times to sustain us until the next reward. We've learned to take it as it comes, though we continually try to manipulate the fates.

Continual optimism abounds within our breed. The ever-present thought that one day we might be blessed with endless flights of willfully decoying birds is the reward for the work. Such optimism cannot be bound by any season.

SHE'S GONE POSTAL

The Marshall family had fallen into the familiar rhythm of another gunning season. The cold winds of November had supplied us with ample birds. Repeated low-pressure cells kept the winds stirring up the bay waters, setting the scene for exceptional hunting opportunities. We had nine box blinds working at the time, and each was providing excellent shooting.

Due to the consistently good hunting that we were enjoying, many "casual" hunters were spurred to take to the blind. On the Eastern Shore, especially around Saxis, many folks had given up the sport. The reasons for it are many but usually revolve around lack of ducks and pressure from "the man." But this year's successes had drawn many of these folks back to the blinds. Five boats were regularly running out of the Jack's Creek Gun Club. Most days, two or more boats would run in the morning and usually one or so in the afternoon. On holidays and weekends, you could bet that all five would be heading out to one blind or another. Local folks wanting to tag along would simply show up at the shop and hop in a boat for a half-day hunt. Local support provides local eyes. Local eyes see everything.

The routine was fairly simple. In the mornings, we'd meet at the shop. Dressing in the warmth of the gas heater, we would pick our blinds for the day, drop the boats in the water and venture forth for the morning's hunt. Depending on the quality of shooting, the phone would usually start ringing about 8:00 a.m. The questions were always the same.

"What time is breakfast?"

"Is she gonna make sausage gravy?"

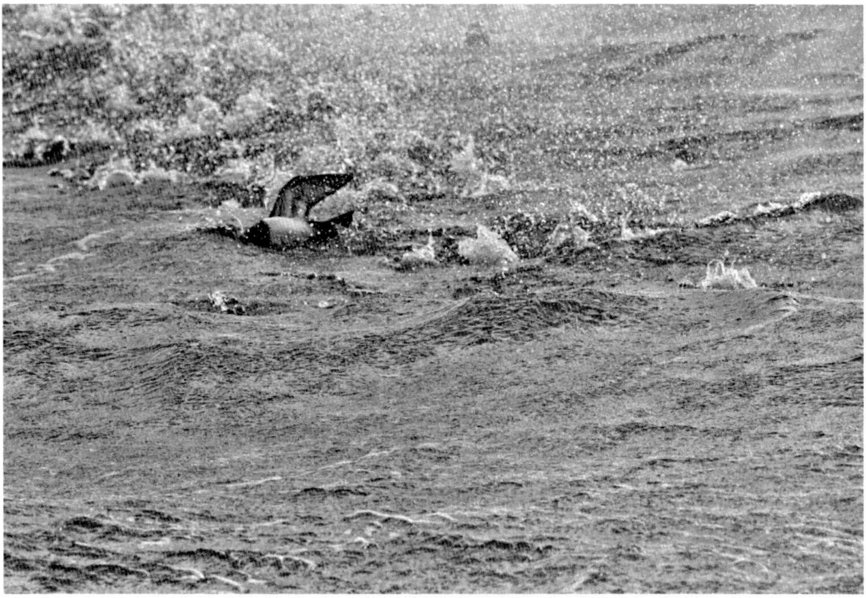

Someone once said that there is nothing quite like a good water swat. In bygone days, it was an effective way to fill the freezer. These days, it ends your day way too quickly. *Paul Bramble photo.*

"Would it be ok if XYZ came along for breakfast this morning?" We'd always pull another chair up to the table.

Time and time again, the questions came in. They were always the same. About 8:30 a.m., I'd place the call to the head chef of the Marshall estate—aka, my mother, Marlene Marshall—to find the answers to these questions and set things in motion. Breakfast at the shop had become legendary. All the food groups were well represented, as long as you liked pork. There'd be bacon, sausage gravy, pork chops, country sausage patties, pancakes, eggs over easy, scrambled eggs with cheese, cathead biscuits, an assortment of homemade jellies and jams, Old Country Time molasses and Chesapeake Bay Farms butter made from only the happiest of cows. At times, our numbers would swell to nearly twenty, our group growing as other hunters "passing by" would see the crowd and drop in. Hunters from eight to eighty share the same table discussing who shot what, who was too hungover to show up, where the law was and where we thought the birds might be. Just the thought of Marlene's breakfast has often been enough to get us through many a slow morning in the box. It had become something that we all looked forward to.

One such morning, Mom was listening to a dozen of us blab on about the aforementioned subjects when she was asked why she had never wanted to tag along on one of our hunts. She confessed that she had been wanting to go for some time, but she knew how we were and wanted to avoid a skirmish with the law. She had put in nearly twenty years of her life for the U.S. Postal service and didn't want to put that in jeopardy by hanging around with a bunch of hardheads like us.

Now she was no stranger to the game. During my college years, she and my father often had to provide support in bushing blinds for the upcoming season. I'd do what I could over the Thanksgiving break, but I'd usually get home for Christmas break about mid-December and jump right into hunting parties. Their help in getting the blinds ready was crucial. I've heard that she and my father had many interesting discussions while cutting and pulling on cedars in the marshes while I was swilling beer down in sunny North Carolina.

She finally succumbed to the peer pressure and, on sunny Saturday afternoon, agreed to join us. Dressed warmly in a pair of coveralls, she boarded the skiff and took the short trip to the blind. In her fur-lined boots, she stepped out of the boat with Dad and began to ready the blind for action. My Chesapeake retriever remained in the boat as I set a small spread of cans and bluebills in front of the blind. Just upwind and at the mouth of a small sandy gut, I placed four black ducks. I'd seen those orange-legged critters hanging out there on a regular basis. There must have been an artesian well or something. On the downwind side, I dropped four hand-carved Bufflehead decoys, having a pretty good idea that we would have some visitors of the small, straight-flying variety that would provide my mother a little bit of fun. Before I got back to the blind, our black-and-white-feathered fowl had begun to come and go at a leisurely pace. Things were looking up.

Upon settling in the blind, we began to familiarize the old girl with the Remington 1100 twenty-gauge semiautomatic that she'd be wielding. Prior to loading it for her, we went over the safety, proper operation of the gun and what to do after the shot. I tossed a crab pot cork off into the water. The light northwest breeze combined with the falling tide began to gently move the target offshore. Pretending to load her gun, I handed it back to her and asked her to shoot the drifting cork. As expected there was a huge flinch as she pulled the trigger. She had expected huge recoil, but there was none. After a few stern looks, some admonishment and a few other choice words, she made certain to watch me put the three Remington Nitro No. 2s into the gun. She then fired two successive shots into the cork, put two more shells in the gun, sat down on the bench and asked for a hot chocolate.

Now ready for action, we sat and waited. It was amazing how much she'd picked up over the years by just by listening to the chatter of gunners gathered around the table. She'd picked up on what was killed on various tides and found it fascinating that we could identify the various species by their flight patterns. Our chatter was interrupted by a pair of buffleheads low to the water and coming directly to our decoys. I let them land just outside the decoys. She rose and shot, but both escaped without harm. It was evident that she was enjoying herself, and it was good to see. Thankfully, it didn't take long for a second opportunity.

Coming from the waters of the open bay, the small flock of four rounded the point and turned in unison as they spotted our decoys. With fast and direct flight, the four came up to one hundred yards. Crossing that mark, they gained a bit of altitude. It was clear that these birds had visited this location before and were fixin' to fall in there again. There was no circling as the four met the water just outside the decoys. It presented a perfect opportunity for Mom to claim her first duck. Pushing water ahead of their fat breasts, they make quick headway to the decoys. Mom, standing in the box with her gun

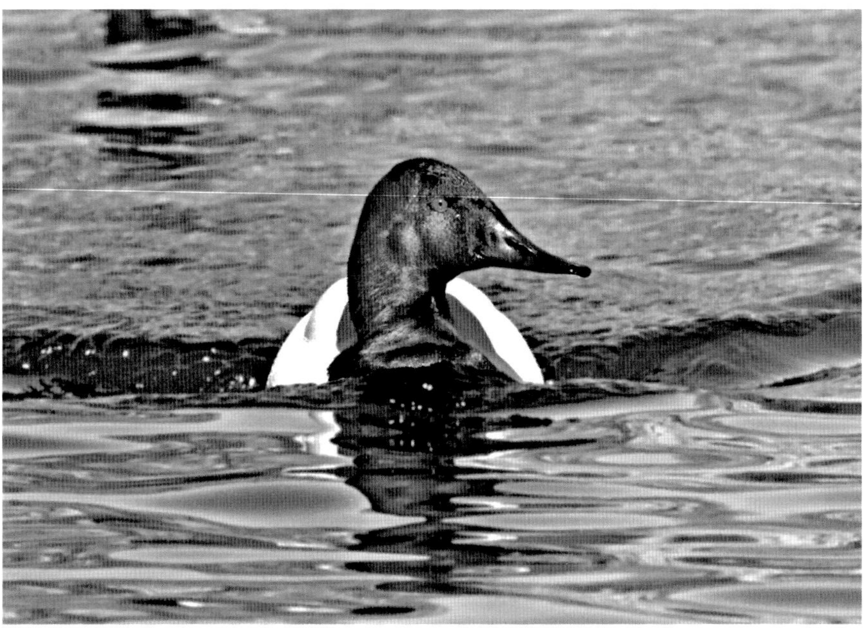

Swimming into the decoys with a purpose, this drake canvasback became my mother's first duck. *Paul Bramble photo.*

shouldered, was obviously nervous. The "swim in" had allowed her time to think. Dad and I just grinned at each other, hoping that everything worked out. Their auburn-colored heads and sloped black bills shone brightly in the afternoon sun. Though the season on them was closed, this opportunity was one that we would not pass up. Three of the invaders stopped at the outside decoy, but a young drake continued unabated into the center of the spread, directly in front of the blind.

Whispering, we gave her the green light to take the closest bird. She acknowledged that she saw it and was ready. The click of the safety heightened the Chesapeake's senses. He could see the ducks, and he saw the gun shouldered and knew that soon he would be called on to do his job. Her first shot rolled the closest drake. There was no second shot.

Her first duck was a fat drake canvasback. I remained silent as Dad gave her a congratulatory hug and welcomed her to the ranks of the "outlaw gunners." She has never let us forget it.

HE WHO HESITATES

The two geese did the unexpected. Cupped and committed, they should have followed the pattern of the previous visitors. But rather than sliding into the decoys on the downwind side of the offshore blind, these two slid to the back of the blind, leaving no shot for the anxious gunners. Seated farthest away from the action, shucking oysters and clams for a midmorning snack, I had no plans to be involved in this shot. Our guide for the day, Steve Barnes, dropped his call to let us know that the two geese were swinging around the back of the blind.

The protective shucking glove and oyster knife were quickly replaced by the old 1187 in my hands. Searching for the incoming pair through the overhanging pines, my son and I spotted them directly overhead. Simultaneously, our guns went up. Two shots rang out in unison. Two geese tumbled cleanly to the water. At that point, my day was complete, not because that goose completed my limit, but because in those four or five seconds, many things were confirmed. My youngest had learned this craft well. He understood how the hunt was supposed to be done and was very capable in the necessary skill set.

But this day was about much more than the shooting. We were participating in the Easton Church of God's annual goose hunt. On the surface, it is quite an amazing event. Over 700 hunters handled by 150 guides take to fields and water over some of the most coveted goose hunting properties across the Upper Shore counties. A morning hunt is followed by a lunch of locally available delicacies, including oysters, fish and venison. Prizes are given away, and a powerful message is delivered by one of the organizers, Billy Hughes. Proceeds from the event fund the Nicholas Bramble Ironman Foundation. Bramble, an outstanding young man, athlete and Christian, died of leukemia in 2004 at the age of twenty. The scholarship provides educational opportunities for deserving area students.

A casual conversation at the Pocomoke Boat Docking Challenge led to my first involvement with this endeavor. On my subsequent trip, I asked a lifelong friend, Don Porter Sr., to tag along. Don, aka "Greater Porter," shares the same addiction to waterfowl hunting that I do. His game of choice is geese. He would rather shoot a pair of geese than fifty ducks. As I told him about the event, it was evident that he was in, so we made our plans. His son, Little Donnie (aka "Lesser Porter"), and grandson would attend as well.

Knowing Don Sr.'s love for goose hunting, the night before we'd planned to play a little trick on the unsuspecting fellow. Our guide played a very important part in setting the stage.

Having been previously versed in how the day would go by our guide, I began complaining about the severity of the boat ride we would be facing immediately upon our 4:00 a.m. departure from Pocomoke. Meeting the balance of our group in Cambridge, we were soon on our way. In the predawn meeting of how the day's hunt would go, our guide played his part in the hoax well. He explained that goose hunting had been very poor and that at about 10:30 a.m., we would have the opportunity to hunt a flooded regulated shooting area. He laid it on thick, explaining that we'd have the chance to possibly see a spoonbill, and most likely some tame mallards would walk by. As he spoke, the noise of hundreds of geese on the nearby creek echoed in the background, but we wouldn't be able to hunt those. Don Sr.'s face was growing longer by the second. He desperately wanted to hunt geese. The more despondent he became about the "chance to see a spoonbill," the thicker Steve laid it on. After about four of the longest minutes he'd spent in a long time, we confessed the ruse and trekked to the skiff for the boat ride. The trip to the blind wasn't all that bad. He took it well.

Arriving at the blind, it was pleasing to see that the rig had already been tied. It numbered over two hundred floater goose decoys. Upon settling in, we began shooting, starting quickly with a suicidal single. For the next two hours, it was a constant flow of sausage, egg and cheese burritos; hot ham and cheese foldovers; cheddar cheese and jalapeño venison summer sausage; hot coffee; and the occasional raw oyster or clam adorned with white balsamic vinegar. A few times, our gastronomic adventure was interrupted by a passing goose.

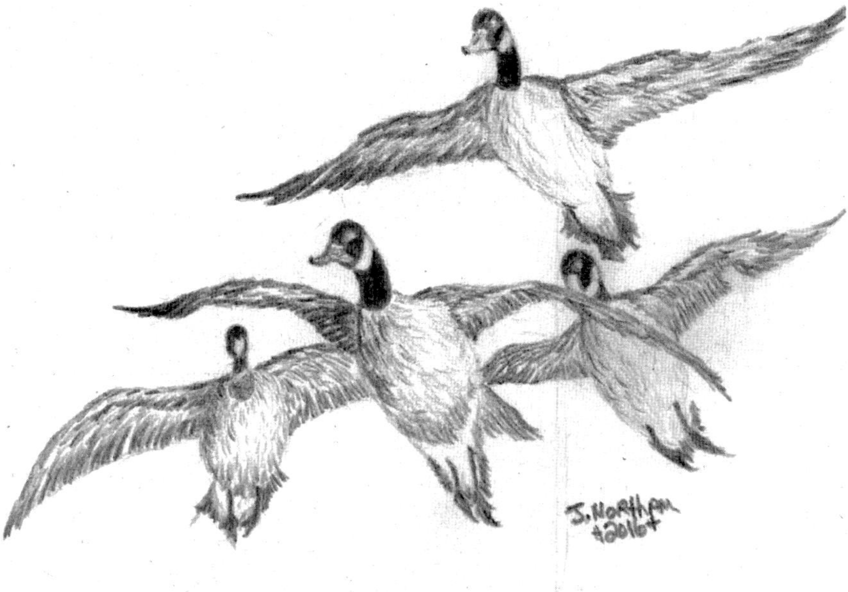

As the morning wore on, we all took our turn on the gun, and a few geese fell. My son Parker had spent most of the morning calling, chasing cripples and shooting the bull with the others in the blind. He lacked one to fill his two-bird limit. Having three generations of Porters in the blind provided all the ammunition we needed to keep spirited conversation going all morning. Donnie Jr., with whom I share a blind on regular occasions, caught the brunt of Parker's barbs. They were well deserved due to his lack of shooting skill on this day.

The construction of our blind for the day was quite unique. With the structure's three-sided configuration, the back was open for the boat to enter. As you stepped out to starboard on the landing platform, the blind was up four steps. On the port side of the boat was an elevated storage area on the same level as the blind, with the boat and landing platform some four feet below. The storage area, now devoid of decoys, made an advantageous observation deck and quite a nice shooting platform on birds that finished behind the blind.

As the morning's endeavors were about to come to a close, a single goose signaled his interest. After considerable coaxing, he committed to the spread and approached the downwind side of the blind, where Donnie Jr. awaited his next turn on the rail. As the bird descended toward the decoys, I watched as Donnie patiently waited for his shot. His gun hung momentarily in a small

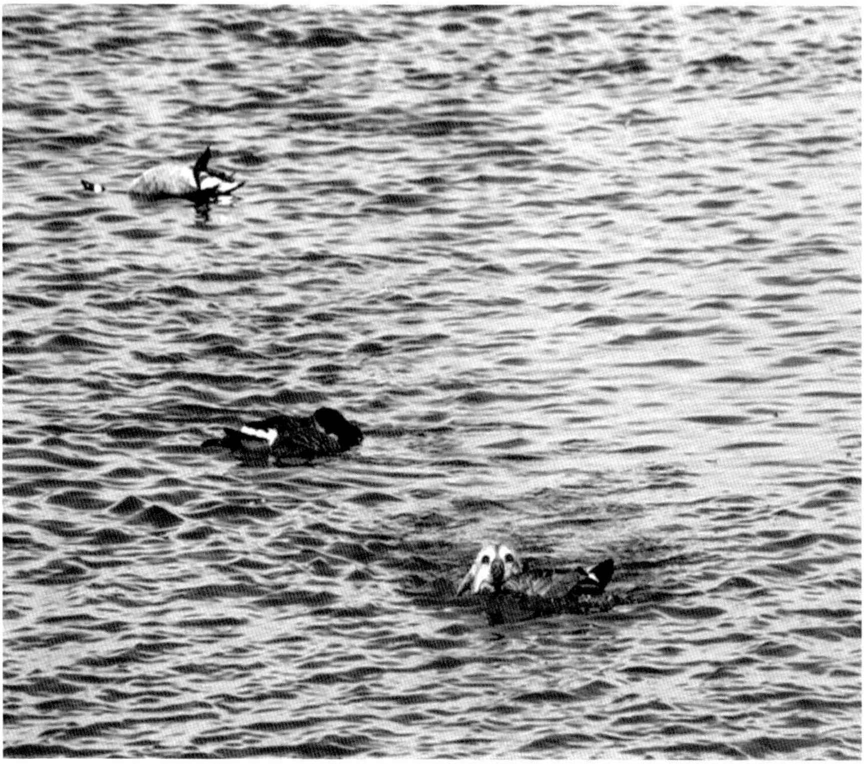

There's nothing quite as pleasing as watching a good dog work. With three geese down, it's quite a luxury not to have to worry about getting after them in the boat. *Paul Bramble photo.*

piece of brush on the blind, and in that moment of hesitation, a single shot rang out, crumpling the goose and sending it to the water. Parker had been standing on the back deck, watching the spectacle take place. When he saw the hesitation, he felt it necessary to shoot, closing the deal nicely. Donnie was left staring down the barrel of his gun at a dead goose.

The discussions that followed are the stuff that good, memorable hunts are made of. Long behind me are the days where the success of a hunt is measured by the number of birds retrieved. There are many factors that compose a good hunt. The people, the scenery and each new sunrise are reasons enough to put in the work.

The events of the latter part of this hunt will make good fodder to use during future trips. I'm sure it will be discussed. And I'm quite certain that Donnie won't make the same mistake again.

LAST RITES

With every swing of the pick, a new memory comes to mind: the way he was curled up in the newspaper basket on that early Christmas morning, the first hunting trip, the good and bad times. But foremost were memories of the unconditional love that dominated his fourteen-year life.

Now, as the grave is being dug, my lab is on the way to the vet. It would be his last ride in the truck that he so eagerly hopped into all those misty November mornings. Upon his return, the wag of his tail will be no more.

Probably the greatest sorrow concerning the loss of a pet is the absence of companionship that always follows. The times where advantage was taken of the dog always comes to mind. Times when your friend's best interest is not near the top of the list of priorities that accompanies any outing. Too many times, emotions are the fuel for poor behavior directed at the animal. Regardless of discipline, hard work or loud vocal instruction, the dog was always ready and willing to give and receive unconditional love.

It is the little things that are missed during the first few days of loss. In the corner by the fridge where his food and water bowls used to sit, things are now quiet. Gone are the training days, walks in the woods and scouting boat rides on the bay.

Somehow, in mid-September, usually with the arrival of the first temperature dip, retrievers sense that it is "their" time of the year. You can see it in their eyes; they know what's about to happen. Hunting season is just around the corner. Though this fourteen-year-old pup was virtually blind due to cataracts, his desire to join the hunt would still rekindle that fire from time to time. It wouldn't burn for long, but it was still in him just the same.

As the topsoil was shoveled away from the hardened clay, stratum was revealed. This sometimes comes away rather easily, but here, the roots of a nearby pine tree made passage difficult. That's fitting. The earliest years were the easiest for my lost friend, and as the years wore on, things got increasingly difficult.

The first thing that threatened his health was the two times he darted in front of passing cars. Both times, he was trying to greet me as I returned from fishing trips. Luckily, neither resulted in serious injury to either party involved. From that point, things seemed to go downhill. He developed epilepsy. Violent convulsions followed that were treated with daily medication. His daily prescriptions grew to eleven pills a day.

Admittedly, he wasn't much of a gun dog. Rather, he offered a quiet companionship that knew no boundaries. I vividly remember times spent clamming, with him running free over the entirety of the flat. I always welcomed his daily greetings in the driveway, though they calmed in intensity as age crept up on him.

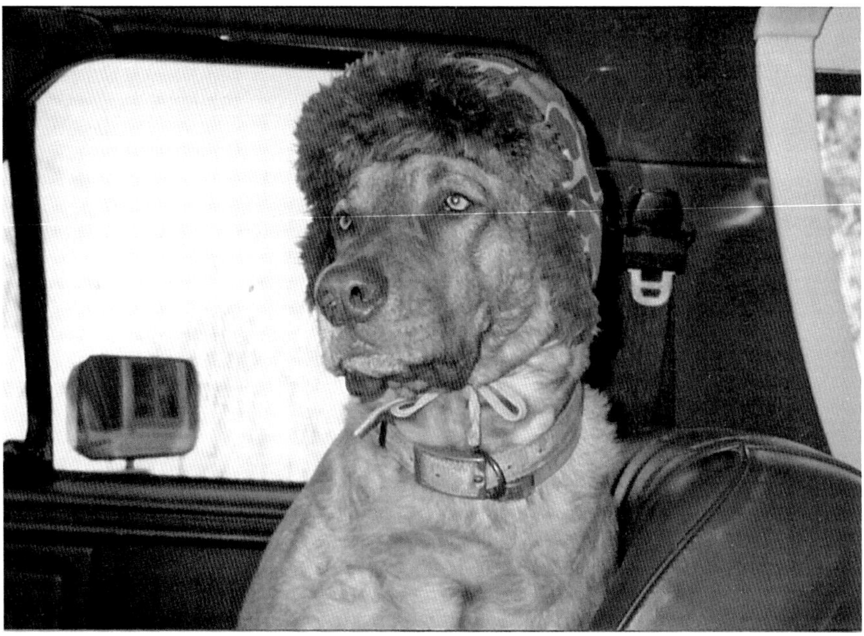

There are many sides to a good hunting dog. Butler didn't seem to mind having to wear the occasional fur-lined hunting hat. *C.L. Marshall photo.*

While I was away at school and at work, I missed the dog much like family. In fact, he was part of the family. As he grew older, I often expected to hear via telephone that my old boy had gone to the western sky. Countless times, I left the house wondering if he would still be alive upon my return, but the old boy hung in there. He was a tough bird.

Anyhow, the point of the matter is that people who opt to be dog owners must face the reality that they will have to go through this ritual several times in a lifetime. It's never easy. What is hard to decide is when, if necessary, to have the animal's life extinguished. Debate over this practice in humans is ongoing, but with pets it's no question.

Folks say that when the pet is incapable of carrying on life in a pain free, self-sufficient way, it is time to have the animal euthanized. On the surface, this seems harsh. It seems cruel. Factually, it does all parties involved a favor. Our much-beloved pet is now free of his suffering, and as owners, we are free of the burden of the dependent animal. Hard though it may be, it is the right course of action, a small consolation when we are left with a void in our lives that was once filled with such love, such promise and such satisfaction for nearly a decade and a half. We knew how it would end when we signed on as the dog's owner. The dog will be part of our lives. We will be all of theirs.

Regardless of the past, the satisfaction that one dog brings only makes us long for another—another dog, another companion, another set of experiences. Often it's different variations of the same theme. Any way you look at it, it's a winning proposition and a rewarding one at that.

PORK CHOPS IN SOUTH CHESSCONESSEX

The reasons we hunt waterfowl are many. Some who hunt alone like the solitude; others enjoy the unique landscape and wonders of nature that occur on most every hunt. For many, it's the social aspect. Unlike other popular types of field sports, waterfowl hunting can be a very social sport. That's one of the things that sets us apart from others sitting in a tree.

The call came in from area celebrity chef Johnny Mo that he'd found a field that was holding geese and that he had gained permission for us to hunt there. Relatively new to hunting, he had the desire and found the geese, but he lacked the gear required to do it right. As I queried him about the situation, he acknowledged that it wasn't just a few geese but rather about three hundred that had been seen frequenting this cornfield in downtown South Chessconessex. I had yet to see the field or the geese. By the excitement in his voice, I could tell that Mo had found something worthwhile. I took his word for it, and he asked for me to call in the "A Team." I immediately set things in motion: made the calls to line up the hunters, loaded the decoy trailers and prepared all the necessary paraphernalia. We made plans for a morning and possibly an afternoon hunt.

For a newbie, Mo had done an excellent job of scouting. We set up in a thin strip of gums that separated two fifty-acre cornfields. They'd been using the one farthest from the road, and due to the wet conditions, we had to carry some of the gear about seventy-five yards from the nearest access road to the spot we selected to hunt. The soft, thawing ground made travel difficult, and the weight of the decoy bags didn't make it any easier. Hastily

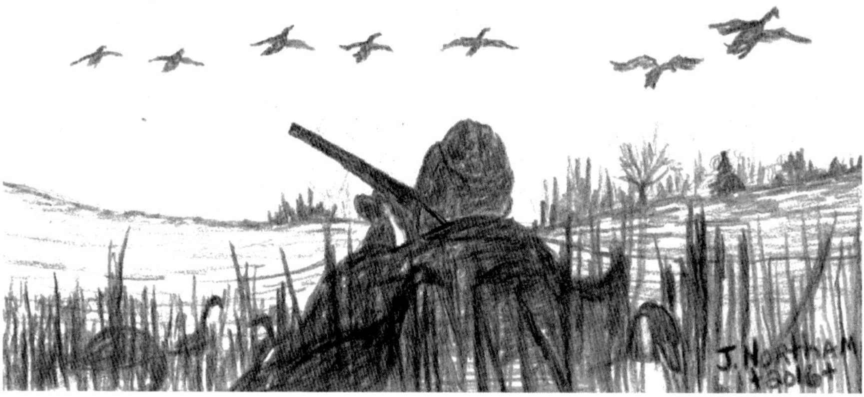

the decoys were set. The light north wind would provide us with right-to-left shooting on decoying birds. We allowed a nice pocket for decoying birds to funnel into at about thirty yards.

The strip of woods provided basic cover, and making good use of materials at hand, we fashioned a pretty good blind. It was large and very comfortable. A nice windbreak was provided by the brush behind us. The folding lawn chairs provided very comfortable seating, and the hard sand of the dry creek bed was firm underfoot. We fashioned a small "coffee table" out of some pine stumps and an old piece of two-by-twelve. Waiting for the geese to fly, we continued to perfect our blind. The charcoal grill provided much-needed heat.

At about 7:30 a.m., the first arrivals settled into pocket. After that, we continued to pick away at small flocks for the next hour. It was clear that we were going to limit out very quickly. Calls went out for more hunters, but they were unsuccessful. There was no cellphone reception in downtown Chessconessex. Driving out of town until reception was gained, I recruited a couple gunning buddies from Saxis, plus a few of the other usual suspects. They arrived very quickly. We hastily added an extension on our hide. Our numbers grew to ten.

Recent weeks of near zero temps had the Chesapeake frozen solid. It was too thick to break through with our outboards and also too thick to worry about going oyster dredging. With the pressures of work allayed, we all were very much at ease. To pass the time and feed our hungry crew, I produced a pork loin from my gunny sack. I'd picked it up the day prior at Matthew's Market in Mappsville, Virginia, and had Bruce slice it in half-inch chops. The sound the seasoned meat made hitting the hot grill was pleasing and fueled our hunger. The first batch came off; each chop was placed between two slices of Wonder bread and quickly dispersed to a waiting crew. Smoke from the chops swirled through the trees as a trio of geese made a sneaky final approach to the decoys. Those with pork chop sandwiches in hand were in no position to shoot. Those without tidily handled the chore. I just continued to grill more sandwiches.

The smoke from the grilled pork chops didn't seem to bother the geese. Because of the smoke, I'd moved the grill to the downwind side of the blind. Looking up from my duties, I gave a few clucks on the Eastern Shoreman, and five more were locked up en route. With three Saxis Islanders on the downwind side of the blind, those five didn't stand a chance. Donnie Porter, Bill Bailey and I cleaned them up nicely. They were followed by two more, which the father-and-son team of Morrisons finally pulled down.

It's no secret that good shooting contributes to a good hunt, but this was one that just sticks in the memory: ten of us, lined up in a long hedge row, laughing, joking, smacking our lips on freshly grilled pork chops and occasionally pulling the trigger on a goose. Plus, it was a cast of characters. This trip was made memorable by a number of things. First, it was unexpected and somewhat on a whim. The thrill of hunting a new area also played a role. Anytime geese are willing participants, it's a good thing. But it was the camaraderie of old and new friends sharing a day together free from the encumbrances of everyday life that made it special. Such days are very few and far between.

I'm glad we got to share that one.

SOLITUDE

Waterfowl hunting can be a very social endeavor. When I reflect on past hunts, I usually find it's the people and experiences that make most trips memorable. Good hunting partners are hard to find, and once folks start gunning together, there's a bond that can last a lifetime. When you decide to gun with someone, it's not a relationship that's entered into lightly. It's far different from just hunting with someone.

Making this decision requires divulging many things that most outsiders will never see. Punctuality, honesty and the ability to keep information private are some of the more important character traits that gunning partners must possess. Boat-handling skill, marksmanship and gear fall somewhere down the line but not necessarily in any specific order. There's no replacing experience, however.

Throughout a hunting lifetime, avid hunters will likely share a blind with hundreds of folks. Some will get the invitation to return, and some will not. But the number of true "gunning partners" one has is far fewer. Often, they can be counted on one hand.

The social aspect of waterfowl hunting is attractive to many. But there are times when the solitude of the sport is a very beautiful thing. Time spent alone on the water is rejuvenating. Throughout my life, there have been periods when I needed time alone, needed to feel the salt air, needed the solitude of the hunting experience.

Just out of Elon College, I'd moved to Harrisonburg, Virginia, for a job. Living in the Shenandoah Valley was thrilling for a while. I'd met some good folks who had taken the time to show me the area and some pretty damn good hunting opportunities. New activities to take up my time and money included bow hunting and turkey hunting. I'd even started freshwater trout fishing. It was on one of these trips that I made the decision to move back to the Shore.

We had run across the mountain on Route 33, past Reddish Knob and into wild, wonderful West Virginia. On some creek whose name I can't remember, we were fishing for rainbow and brown trout. On about the third cast, I hooked and landed one of about three pounds. My partners were quite excited about the size of the fish. I just looked at it, thinking that back home, I'd be using something of this size for blue marlin or shark bait. Staring down at this fish lying on the brown river rock, I decided to move back to the Eastern Shore. I put in my notice the following day. With it came a multitude of decisions and the most pressure I'd ever had to deal with. I longed to spend time in the blind. I needed time with my old gunning partner.

Upon my return to the Shore, the things that make up a life were piling up fast. There was a house to buy, a marriage proposal pending and a new job to deal with. The pressure was starting to get to me. I needed to go hunting. But this time, I needed to go alone.

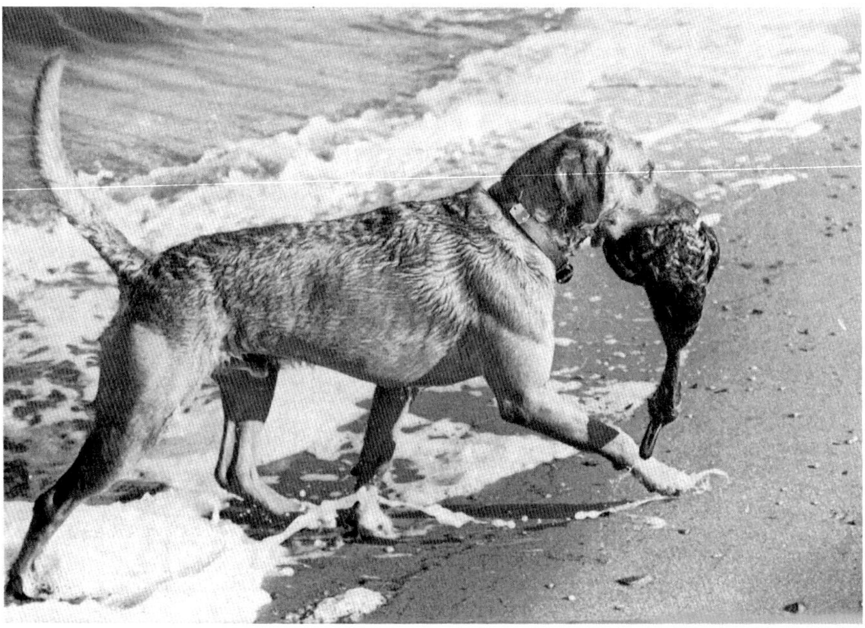

Sanford's Sir Butler proudly strides ashore with a fat black duck. Not wind, nor waves nor ice failed to prevent him from getting his job done. *C.L. Marshall photo.*

The morning was out. There was just too much stuff to deal with. At about one o'clock, I broke free and ran, looking for the serenity of my box up Cattail Creek. It is a place I know well. I've hunted there now for forty years. It's ground zero.

Every part of the trip was therapeutic on this day. The familiarity of the process was very comforting. Launching the boat, the ride out Messongo Creek, through Rock Gut, across Cattail Channel and up Cattail Creek was smooth and blissful. There was comfort in the ritual of setting out the three dozen Canada geese floaters. Running the boat in the skiff blind, I grabbed my gun and bag and lackadaisically walked across the island to the blind. Tossing my gun and bag in the box, I decided to linger outside the blind for a while. The enjoyable stroll around the small island yielded six or so oysters. I had a plan for them in the near future.

The blind was well bushed and concealed me well in a standing position. As the sun began to fall to the west, the wind began to fall out. It was a beautiful afternoon, light winds and temps in the high forties. There wasn't much moving, so I just stood facing out of the back of the blind, admiring the view of the area. Finally, my mind had cleared from all the crap that had been running through it. The solitude of the afternoon was refreshing. There's no telling how many birds came and went from the spread while I was in a little world of my own.

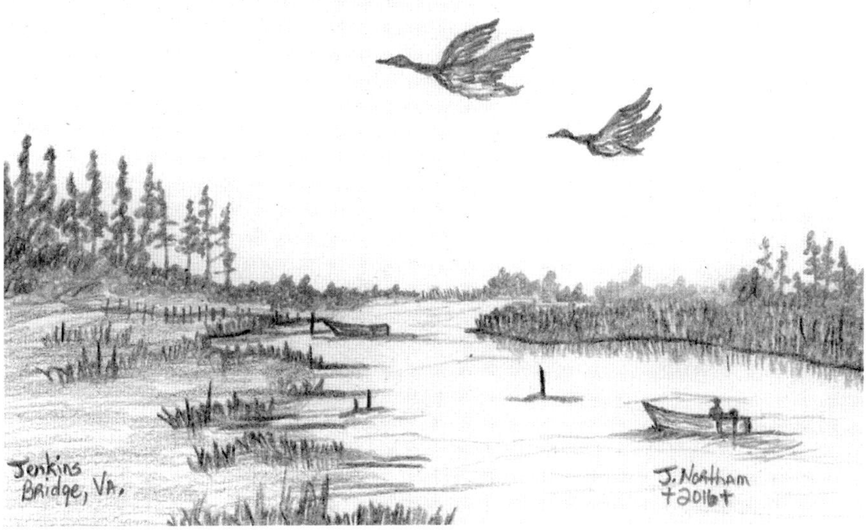

My solitude was broken by the distinctive sound of wind rushing through feathers. It sounded close. My first instinct was to turn quickly, but I resisted. Slowly, I picked up the Browning with my left hand and turned to the right. At twenty-five yards, suspended atop the landing zone, was a pair of geese. They had come in without a sound. With the instinct of my forefathers, I shouldered the gun, and then the pair lay feet up in the decoys.

The tide had slowed, the wind had died and it was an absolutely stunning sunset. In solitude, I watched the last of the sun slip below the horizon of the Pocomoke Sound. In no particular hurry, I picked up the decoys and the pair of geese and made my way home in the darkness.

SPRING-FED WOODROWS

The early teal season doesn't do a lot for us on the Eastern Shore. It's not until the second split that we get a good influx of summer ducks. For us, it's usually wood ducks that we target in the muddy marshes along the banks of the Pocomoke River.

We'd scouted out a spot over the previous couple weeks. I had found a few ducks on a secondary creek off the Pocomoke. It offered a shallow, muddy bank, a smaller feeder creek off to the south and a place where, on each visit, we'd found wood ducks. It just seemed like a spot where they liked to be. But scouting it and hunting it are two very different things.

It's purely a public hunting experience, first come, first served. In order to claim our desired spot, my youngest son, Parker, and one of his buddies took one for the team by going to the ramp at 3:00 a.m. Three others had launched before him, and he had to wait on the fourth. Luckily, the four other rigs hadn't stumbled on our honey hole, and he was able to claim it. At the leisurely hour of 6:00 a.m., we met him at the dock while his friend Jake held our spot. Bobby Graves, David Graham, my golden retriever Gunner and I just stepped aboard like city slickers, and we were off.

The decoys were quickly set as we'd discussed the night before. By the time we got the boat hidden and back to the blind, several groups had already tried to fall in that little creek. It looked promising. The countdown to legal shooting began, and as if on cue, a pair fluttered over the Mojo right at legal. We shot steadily for the next hour, though not particularly well. Our

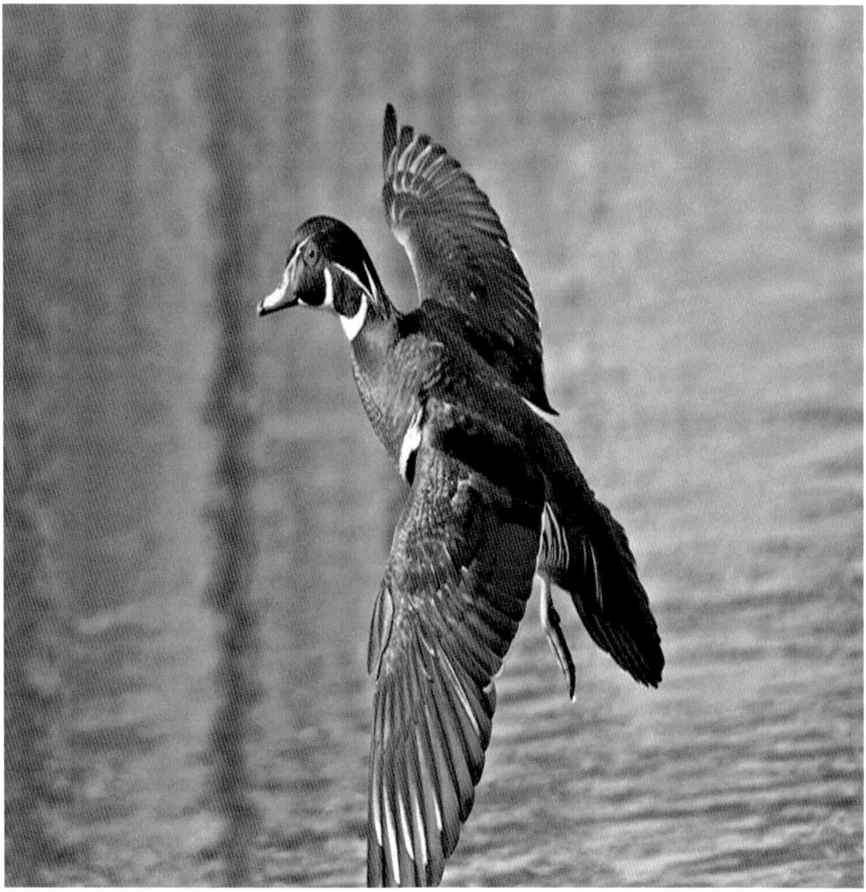

The tannic acid–stained waters of the Pocomoke River provide a perfect habitat for wood ducks. In the early morning, their low, direct flight pattern often works in the hunter's favor. *Paul Bramble photo.*

scouting had paid off, as we seemed to be provided with the majority of the action in that relatively small marsh.

By 8:00 a.m., we were four shy of a five-man limit. Things had slowed as we watched four avoid our decoys and fall in a couple bends up the creek. They were only about sixty yards from us but well hidden from sight. With the mischievous look of a teenager, Bobby set out to craw down on them. Now, Bobby is quite a hunter but no longer a spring chicken. Prior to letting him leave, odds were set for a variety of outcomes, bets were made and there was some rather spirited discussion. All occurred, of course, in hushed voices.

From our vantage point, we reckoned correctly that we'd be able to see the whole thing. He slid out of the blind like a marsh ninja. The ducks were only sixty yards away, but it would require a fifty-yard stalk to get them in range, if they hadn't swum up the creek. The first twenty yards were easy, after that he was commando-crawling through the marsh until he reached the first bend in the creek. At that point, he stopped his slither. The quarry had drifted toward us riding the outgoing tide. By the look of things, we expected him to shoot at any moment. Then things took a very interesting turn.

Bobby's an old-school hunter. He knew we were four shy, and he was going to try to get them right there. We watched in amazement as he purposely began to unscrew the magazine cap of his Remington 1100. He silently slipped off the forearm and set it aside. Using his pocket knife, he pushed and turned off the magazine plug. As he began to pull it, out the magazine spring launched nearly five feet in the air, coming to rest in a saltwater bush just to his left. From our vantage point, we could plainly see this whole drama unfolding. It was truly amazing how he held it together and didn't spook the ducks that now were just thirty yards from him.

Now limited to a "one shot automatic," the chances of the quadruple he was dreaming of, and betting on, were seemingly slipping away. He slowly began looking around for the spring. For five full minutes, we watched him try to find it.

Watching him struggle to find the spring was rather comical. We could see his frustration growing as the wood ducks paddled around unaware of the drama playing out just thirty yards away.

Finally, he reached up to his left, picked the spring from saltwater bush and began to reassemble his gun. It seemed like we were watching this for an hour when, in reality, it took place over a fifteen-minute span. We passed on several groups waiting for this to unfold and not wanting to ruin all the work that Bobby had put into this stalk.

Finally, he got the thing back together. After all of that, he left the plug in. Only two were left in range by the time he was able to shoot. They were picked off, one water swatted and the other on the rise. Gunner was dispatched for the cleanup.

It was an all-time classic marsh-belly-crawl-commando-ninja stalk and one that, when drinks are flowing, always comes up in conversation.

SURVIVORS TALK

I was leaving Rock Hall when the call came in. The Pocomoke Sound was full of diving ducks, and the pending weather would have them leaving the safety of the large water in search of the shelter of a leeward shore. We were to meet later that evening to discuss our plan. I was asked to bring the dog.

"The dog" was my Chesapeake Bay retriever, which we dubbed Butler. From an early age, this hardheaded pup chewed, bit and clawed everything that came in his way. His affinity for the water was obvious; it seemed as though he thrived in the muddy headwaters of Jacks Creek on a daily basis. My skill at bathing him grew.

He hadn't come from a hunting family, and we knew nothing of how to pick a good retriever. He was picked from the litter because he was the lightest in color, boasting a champagne coat among the curly chestnut-haired siblings. The dog's physical condition was superb, and he learned quickly. He mastered basic commands of sit, stay, load up and get him. It was clear that Butler was to be a one-man dog, and he was as hardheaded as he was loyal.

We worked on basic obedience commands while peeler crabbing in the shallow waters off Saxis. Poor behavior resulted in him being tossed over and forced to swim while I fished a few pots. The distance of one hundred or so yards two or three times a morning tuned his obedience skill and quickly added muscle to his lean frame. He was developing into quite a specimen.

One hot early June day, it was becoming evident that double crabs were coming on the full moon. I'd saved a couple bushels of jimmies and sat in Aldon Miles and Sons Crab house along with brothers Ralph and Aubrey

Miles. By holding the claws together and gently bending them back by the "elbows," the jimmies would release their claws. As such, these declawed jimmies were placed in the upstairs of the peeler pots and would lure the females into the pot. Butler lay on the cool floor of the crab house facing me, his stern toward the door. One of the crabs had eased out of the basket as we worked feverishly to finish our task. With a squeal, Butler hauled ass out of the crab house and spun in tight circles as the jimmy held on tightly to his testicles. Finally, the crab was flung off and quickly felt the wrath of the Chessie. He waited outside for me from that day on.

Though I shot hundreds and hundreds of ducks over this dog, it was the aforementioned day on William's Point that sticks out the most. The plan was set the night before and, if well executed, would yield huge dividends. These flocks of birds would be looking for food and shelter in the forecasted high northwest winds. The last two hours of rising tide and first two of the ebb would make our hunt much easier.

The alarm went off at 3:30 a.m. Easing into the kitchen, I set the coffee in motion prior to doing anything else. Thirty minutes later, the skiff hit the water loaded with several dozen canvasback decoys, two dozen floater geese and a dozen full-body field goose stools. The ride out of the Pocomoke River was interrupted by wind-whipped salt spray and sharp jolts against the hull made by waves as we broke into the open water of the sound. Thankfully, it was a short run.

As I nosed the boat up on the beach, my hunting partner drew the anchor tight and began the task of making our hide. We dug two rough pits in the sandy spit about eighteen inches deep and each large enough for our layout blind to snuggle nicely in. Sand was sprinkled atop the blinds. We would be virtually invisible to the coming ducks and had no worries of being flooded out, as the tide was due to turn in just ninety minutes. The dog waited on the beach as we set the decoys. The divers were set in a traditional J pattern, with the geese inside and downwind. Several flocks skittered past as we hid the boat downwind a couple hundred yards.

Settling in the layout blinds, we poured cups of hot coffee and anxiously awaited what was about to happen. Midway through it, we had our first visitors. Two of the four pitched before we could get right. There was one survivor. I heard something muttered from the adjoining layout about survivors talking and that there would be no more of that. As I reloaded, Butler was back with the first and turned to the other two that were belly up side by side. He grabbed each by the head and saved a trip.

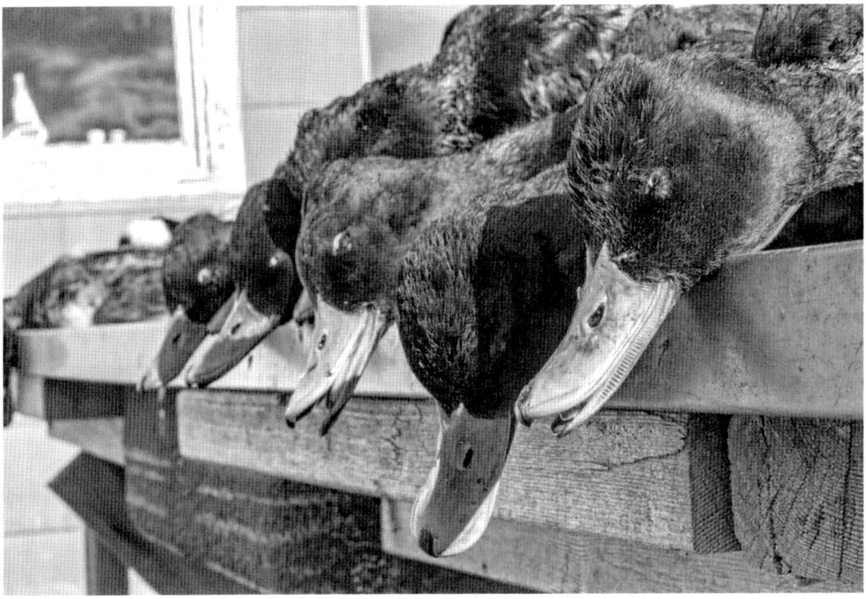

A four-man limit of bluebills marks a stellar hunting day on the Pocomoke Sound. *Paul Bramble photo.*

Tiptoeing across the whitecaps was a flock of twelve geese. They had seen our decoys and had decided to join the party. Lying on my back eyeing the flock as my excited clucks and calls turned into moans and purrs, I heard the safety switch off in the blind beside me. A flock of bluebills lit just outside the decoys, but we lay still. Those geese were on our mind. Their silence told the tale of what was about to happen. They swung in front of us with the wind on their side and slowed greatly as the landing gear went out. My partner's first shot left two down, as did mine. We had done this before and without speaking knew what was expected of each other. Our six shots claimed seven, with two cripples. One was dispatched cleanly as the other swam quickly away with the wind at his back. Butler was in the water as the first cripple was dispatched. We were up and wading out to the seven as Butler pulled off the dead and began chasing the fleeing bird. Calling him off was no use. He wouldn't be denied.

The retrieve seemed to last forever. The goose would dive and resurface a few feet away, and the chase would be rejoined. All the time, it was getting farther and farther from our makeshift pit, riding the strong outgoing current. Watching the life-and-death ordeal play out, I began to move for the boat as the distance now measured nearly a quarter mile. Butler continued on the retrieve. I kept losing sight of him in the building waves. Each new sighting of him was a relief. Finally, I heard an excited yell from my partner's pit. He had spotted him through his binoculars and was tuned in to every move of the dog and the escaping goose. "He's got him! He's on the way back!" I heard him yell as I fired up the Yamaha and eased past the decoys. I couldn't find the dog in the building seas. Through the spray, I finally found him battling the wind, waves and current nearly a half mile from the pits. He had the goose by the neck and had properly dispatched it. Coming along broadside of him, I loaded him aboard the scow like we'd done so many times before in warmer weather. He wouldn't relinquish his grasp on the goose until he was in the boat.

With a combination of ninety pounds of pure Chesapeake muscle and untamed desire, Butler had gone headlong into the roughest conditions that the Pocomoke Sound had to offer. Fighting off current, wind, whitecaps and distance, he had done his job. Back ashore, he took his place and waited for the scene to be replayed again. No doubt, he was ready.

TALES OF A NODAK VIRGIN

According to the magazines and Internet, the North Dakota prairie pothole region appeared to be a duck hunter's paradise. Funnel clouds of descending mallards filled my imagination as I booked the airline tickets. It would be my first trip out west. The tales of waterfowl numbers brought back by my fellow duck hunters in previous years only fueled my excitement. I had to see it for myself.

My gunning partner Anfernee Thomas and I headed to Short Pump to meet Glen "the Assassin" Wadkins and his crew. We loaded his GMC with layout blinds, decoys, kayaks, coolers of food and drink and all the other paraphernalia necessary for an eight-day odyssey in the heartland. The image of him pulling out of the driveway drew a likening to the old *Beverly Hillbillies* truck rolling into Beverly Hills. Sipping on Maker's Mark, we retreated to our hotel in preparation for our flight out the next day.

Landing in Sioux Falls, it was obvious that we had left the population centers of the East Coast. Grabbing our gear and our rental truck for the week, we embarked on the four-hour trip north to Ashley. At a stop by the first liquor store we saw, we acquired a bottle of Evan Williams Single Barrel that would make the trip palpable, and at another stop, by the Cabela's in Mitchell, South Dakota, we gathered some last-minute supplies to make the trip across the barren agricultural land more interesting. Traveling during the daylight hours was pleasant with limited traffic. Once we crossed the slope coming into North Dakota, the landscape became pockmarked by potholes and sloughs, all teeming with waterfowl.

Arriving in midafternoon, we quickly stowed our gear and went out to scout for the morning's hunt. Hunting such large land successfully requires work. Scouting, property maps, knocking on farmer's doors, hours of driving and glassing were all required to make the most out of limited days. With not much time to work with, we elected to hunt the first morning on our host's five thousand acres. We found a slough surrounded by fresh-cut corn that was holding a few hundred mallards. The next morning, we lay in wait for them.

Words cannot express our excitement as we settled into the layout blinds. The wind was at our back, blowing at a steady twenty miles per hour with gusts of up to thirty. The first arrivals were the greenwings. They came in bunches with the first available light. We passed on the first couple flocks, but with growing light, we thought better of it and got down to business. Our first shot came from a flock of thirty. We spied them skipping along the tops of the cattails as their speed slowed significantly to make their final approach into the wind. From that point on, it was a steady flow of fowl of all flavors. In short order, we had a pile of teals, a few mallards, widgeons, redheads and a couple pintails floating against the far bank. Though slow by NoDak terms, we'd accumulated a four-man limit by 9:00 a.m.

We elected to split up and had different directions for our midday scouting. We met in Klum at the appointed hour to discuss our afternoon options. We elected to hunt closer to home that afternoon, saving the mother lode we'd discovered for the next morning. The afternoon hunt yielded some nice shooting on gadwalls and widgeons. The next morning, we had the hunt that dreams are made of. Lying in the corn stubble while thousands of mallards swirled overhead like a tornado, I was satisfied that the time and money spent were worth it, and I hadn't even pulled the trigger.

Some think that hunting out there is easy. From all the magazines, it appears as though you can hunt anywhere, easily take your limit and do it on consecutive days. That is far from the truth. Though the results can be outstanding, it requires hard work. Access to private land is becoming more difficult. More and more of the land is being posted. Being able to take "no" for an answer, long hours scouting and a good sense of direction are keys to NoDak success.

On our last day there, we found a soybean field that held no birds. But it was near a large lake that held thousands of mallards. Along a hedgerow was a depression that held about a fifty- by one-hundred-yard piece of sheet water. Without a doubt, those mallards would find their way there in the minutes that preceded sunset. Setting up with a huge spread of full-body mallards, Canada geese and pintails, we sat for two and a half hours without seeing a bird in the air. Fifteen minutes before sunset, a flock of a dozen sneaked up on us from behind, hooked into the wind and suspended over our decoys. Eighteen shots rang out in rapid succession. There were four survivors.

The next twelve minutes will forever be etched in my mind's eye. The birds fell like rain. There was no stopping these greenheads from coming to that little patch of sheeted water. The action was fast and furious, and we continued our barrage as the sun dipped past the horizon. When the shooting was done, the birds continued to funnel into the decoys. Knowing these were our last minutes of our "hunting dream," we lay silent with guns unloaded drinking beer and watching the events unfold over our decoys. It was an amazing sight, one that will be remembered long after the number of birds bagged fades.

I can't wait to do it again.

THE DAY THE DUCKS WON

Most folks tend to get a little nervous when hunting with someone they have not yet met. I guess that I've done it so much in my life that it's something I actually look forward to. With the advent of the Internet age and "cyber hunting" (gleaning information about good hunting locations from other hunters online when they boast of successes), it's very possible to expand your circle of hunting friends. As I sat and waited at the Cedar Hall dock for our folks to arrive, I wondered just what I had gotten myself into.

About halfway through my cup of coffee, headlights shone brightly entering the parking lot. Those Thomas boys, with another F-150 trailing, made the turn into the parking lot. Backing his boat into the throat of the ramp, Anthony and his father, Butch, jumped out. The trailing truck emptied a short, stout driver and a tall, thin younger fella. I'd chatted with each in various forums about hunting, but in that arena, there's no telling who, or what, you actually connected with. The stout fella, Dennis Lynch, had been fishing out of the Ocean City Fishing Center for a couple years, and that's how Anthony got know him. His buddy Dave Sikorski seemed knowledgeable enough online and would be my hunting partner for the day.

We got the skiff off the trailer, and since Dave and I would have a much longer run, we got underway first. I'd originally planned to hunt closer to home but decided to make a more aggressive play in hopes of finding more ducks. Our plan was to run out of the Pocomoke River, through the Fair Island cut and across the upper reaches of the Pocomoke Sound to East

Creek. There I held a blind stake, the wind was favorable and I hadn't been over there yet this year. Today was as good a day as any.

Sailing at night on the Pocomoke River is always interesting. The high tides invariably float cypress logs out of the swamps. They ride low in the water and can do irreparable damage to a thin-skinned aluminum johnboat or a lower unit. On this moonless morning, my Streamlight scanned the water for any irregularities. Fortunately, none were encountered.

Two bends up from the mouth of the river, I could see the strong spotlight of a Vulcan tugboat. Based on its angle, I could also extrapolate that it was coming upriver. As we rounded the bend near Shelltown, it became clear that we'd encounter the tug and its tow within the cut channel that bisects Fair Island from the mainland. This "shortcut" was made many years ago and shaves nearly an hour off a tug's ride up the river. It also provides sufficient depth that the other passage could not consistently provide. We decided not to navigate the rather small passage with the tug en route and waited just inside Williams Point as it passed. It was obvious that the captain knew of our existence, as he lit us up with his powerful beam as we cut across the river a half a mile in front of him toward the safety inside the cove. Waiting patiently as he passed, we were soon on our way again.

Emerging from the top end of the cut, we poked our nose into the big waters of the sound. I had underestimated the northwest wind that had now stiffened to fifteen miles per hour. We'd have it directly on our nose for the ride across the sound if we held our current course. In an effort to avoid the beating that we were inevitably going to take, I held the boat under bank toward Marumsco Creek for as long as I could. Finding calmer water as we approached the lee created by Tull's Point, I slowed the boat to examine the toll that the crossing had taken. We had taken on quite a bit of water, but nothing that I felt was critical at this point. We decided to deal with it later.

The ride had been much longer and rougher than I had predicted. Rounding Tull's Point, we faced a short whipping until we found the shelter of East Creek. The coming of the new day was signaled by the pink rim on the eastern horizon. We efficiently set our spread with a greater concentration on puddlers than divers. As confidence decoys, we set up a dozen floater goose decoys just outside and a bit upwind of the black duck decoys. The blind was popped up and our guns loaded, and we were ready. A single mallard found the blocks appealing and wound up being the first addition to our bag.

Flying low on the water and coming in from the east, the pair of black ducks had made their decision upon spotting the decoys. There was no

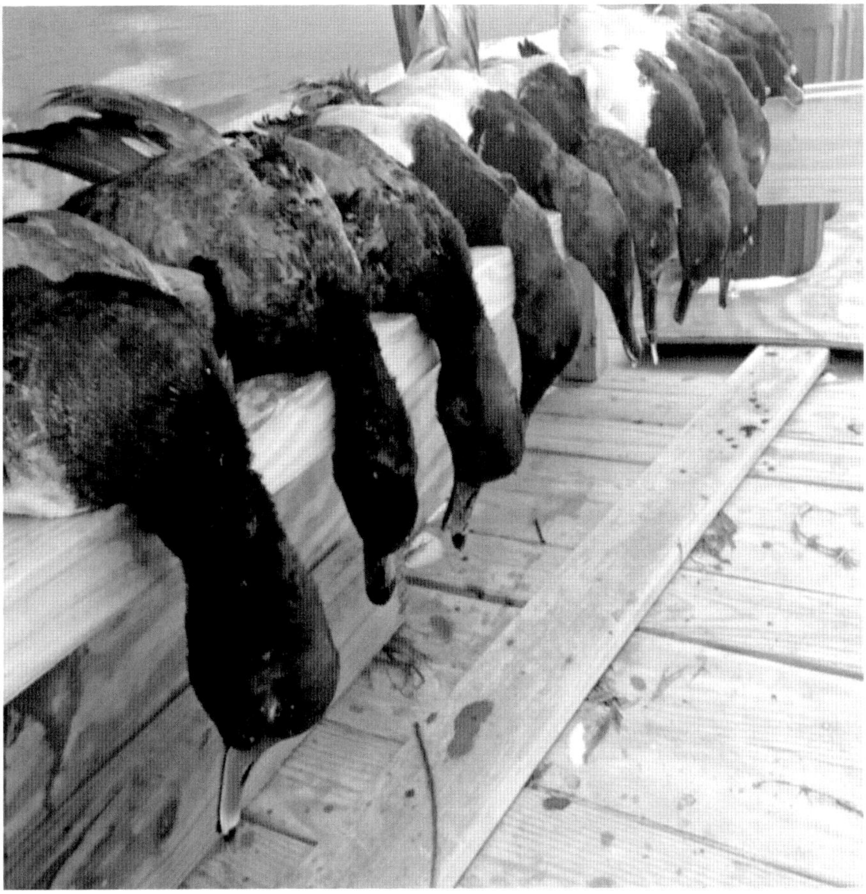

Cans, redheads and bluebills make up a Tangier Sound grand slam. It's a rare occurrence. *Paul Bramble photo.*

circling; no highballs or feeding chuckles were required. Tiptoeing across the waves, the pair simply set their wings and committed to the decoys. They apparently had it on their minds also and wanted to be right up next to the bank. Crossing the outer limits of the decoys, they continued to glide toward us. At twenty-five yards, I called the shot. The two fell simultaneously. A third shot provided the coup de grâce that the drake required. We were off to a good start.

My golden was suffering from a cut pad on his paw and could not make the trip. With these three ducks down, and a considerable amount of water still in the boat, I decided to handle both of these chores. I asked Dave to hop out of the boat and guard the decoys while I picked up the birds and ran the water out of the boat. After stepping out on the sandy bottom, I handed him his Berretta. Using my oak push pole with the wind at my back, I quickly picked up the pair of blacks. From there, I had sufficient depth to operate the outboard. The mallard had drifted nearly one hundred yards from the decoy spread when I found him. It was a very young bird, certainly one from this year's hatch. After I plucked him from the water, I removed the drain plug and brought the skiff up on plane. The collected water rushed to the stern as I made certain that the drain hole was clear. Heading up the creek, I sent a swell toward the decoys, adding movement to them that seemingly brought them to life.

Looking back toward the spread and Dave crouched along the shoreline, I thought our spread looked good. It must have looked good to the three pintails that locked up from an altitude of 150 yards and began a direct descent to the decoys. With Dave's first shot, the drake was killed cleanly. His second shot knocked down a second drake. The third duck, trailing his fallen comrades by twenty yards, made a clean escape. Wading out ten or so yards in the decoys, Dave stopped the second drake's swimming escape with a well-placed load of No. 2s. Seeing that he had the situation under control, I continued to rid the boat of water.

After running about a half mile up the creek, I felt that by turning around now, the run back should take care of the remaining water. About a quarter mile from the blind stake, I cut the engine and replaced the drain plug. There I was witness to a flock of fifty greenwing teal circling once just outside the decoys. On the second pass, they fell right in the decoys, stacking up on the sandbar just thirty yards from Dave's position. Upwind and at a distance of a quarter mile, I should have been able to hear the gun shots that I knew would be forthcoming at any moment. I longed to share this opportunity with Dave. I waited—and waited, and waited—but no shot came. After what seemed like an eternity, I saw Dave stand up, flushing the fifty speedsters from the decoys. Surely, he would shoot now, I thought, but no shot was fired.

Baffled, I fired up the Yamaha, rode slowly past the decoys and picked up two beautiful pintail drakes. In full plumage, their long, slender necks and vermiculated backs were very welcome sights. As I placed them on the center seat, I thought of their mild flavor paired with mushroom gravy and Layton's Chance Vineyard's Farm Red for that night's dinner. But more importantly, why hadn't this fella shot those teal? They were certainly in range. He certainly saw them. This was the first time I'd hunted with this guy. I can appreciate the fact that he may have not wanted to pull the trigger and just observe. We've all done that. But I'd witnessed the fire in his eyes as he waxed that mallard. I saw pure joy when those two blacks were done in. From afar, I saw polished shooting skill as two decoying pintails were nicely handled. Somehow, I didn't think he was just appreciating the scenery.

I decided that I'd let him answer that question when he was ready. As I pulled the boat back into its original position, he tied off the bow line to our stake, and I tossed the anchor off the stern and pulled the boat tight to the bank. Resetting the blind on the boat, he admired the pintails and then sat down silently on a five-gallon bucket. It was obvious that something had gone wrong. It was also clear that he would be spilling the beans. Pouring us cups of coffee, I just waited. It didn't take long.

After I handed him his cup, he began to talk. When he stepped out of the boat, he'd forgotten to grab his blind bag, which contained his shells. He had none in his pocket, only the three in his gun. Once they were used to bag the pintails, he had run out of ammo. There he stood as fifty greenwing teal came storming into the decoys, knocking goose decoys over, swimming around the black ducks and standing on the shallow sandbar just thirty yards from his position. He could only sit and watch.

Our day continued on as the tide rose and we laughed about his misfortune, though misfortune is not really what it turned out to be. This event provided the basis of many more outdoor adventures across the Mid-Atlantic. We finished our day with a nice knot of bluebills rocketing across

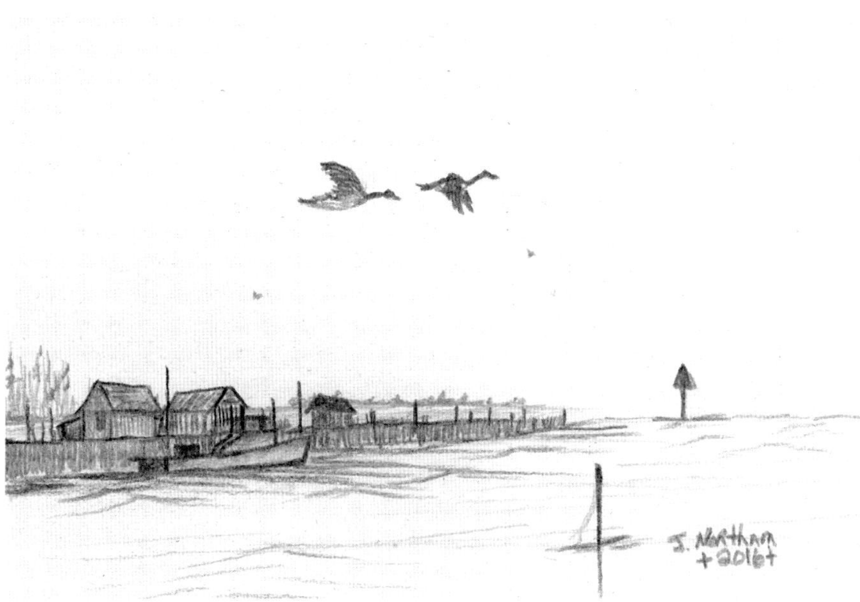

the decoys twice before allowing us the shot we were waiting for. Picking up our decoys, we rode fair wind and fair tide back up the river.

The shot that he was unable to take provided more opportunity for discussion than any water swat could ever promote. It was certainly something that could have happened to any hunter, especially when hunting with a new partner and in a new location. It also goes to prove that often the shot not taken can be the shot most remembered.

LAST TRIP TO PRY COVE

It was an ambitious plan. Having heard the exploits of fellow hunters who had experienced hunting "across the sound," we longed for a similar experience. The decision had been made. The weather would cooperate, and the birds were there. We would make the trip on Saturday morning.

Loading the boat on Friday night took more time than usual. I cut down on the number of divers from what I usually carry. Three dozen would have to do. Geese were limited to an even dozen. A mixed dozen blacks, pintails and bald crowns would round out our rig. Stowed in the bow of the Saxis Island Sportfisherman (a twenty-foot scow) along with the decoys was our pop-up blind, a little covering material and our standard gear. The plan was to keep the load light.

The trip to South Marsh Island from Wenona, Maryland, required a run of about eight miles across the Tangier Sound. There is no rougher patch of water than that crossing on a rising tide and strong northwest wind. This is precisely what I'd be facing in the coming dawn. From what we had heard, there were thousands of divers feeding on the submerged aquatic vegetation. The folks who had made the trip earlier in the week had experienced some of the best shooting in recent years. We wanted our part of it.

Just the week prior, a group had made the trip in a small aluminum johnboat. The weather took a turn for the worse during their hunt. Enjoying a good day of shooting, they stayed a little too long. On the return trip back to Wenona, they caught a crab pot around the prop. Most likely, the boat was stern to the waves, filled up with water and promptly sunk, leaving the group of hunters to perish in the icy waters. Little complications often mushroom into larger and larger issues on the cold, windswept bay. We hoped to avoid such happenings.

The alarm went off at the ungodly hour of 3:00 a.m. Stumbling into the kitchen, I launched the coffee switch into gear, sending a steady stream of caffeinated goodness into the carafe. After I gathered my clothes, I filled the Stanley thermos, grabbed the hip boots from beside the furnace and fired up the old truck. I met my gunning partner at Goose Creek in Westover. We loaded fuel and snacks aboard, and then we were on our way.

As we idled out of the harbor, the waypoint was set. Our route would take us on a southerly course around Sheepshead Point, skirting the Western Islands, and along Oyster Cove. Having never been to South Marsh, I elected to take it easy as we traveled at eighteen knots through the darkness. Upon reaching the first turn of our route just off Muscle Hole Point, I was finally able to make out the faint outline of the island. There was a feeling of relief at having the passing behind me. I slowed the boat on the leeward side of the island and idled toward Pry Island. As the beam of the hand-held spotlight lit up the remnants of Pry Island, we made the decision to venture up onto Pry Cove for a look. The cove was shallow and sandy, with spotty grass scattered throughout. It looked like prime speckled trout waters, but that would have to wait for another day.

We decided to tie our rig on Johnson's Point. At the entrance to this huge food-filled cove, the point created a windbreak that was a welcomed respite for travel-wary waterfowl. Nosing the skiff up on the bank, we unloaded our blind, covering materials, gunning bags and weapons. I set about tying the rig as my partner rigged the blind. I elected to put the divers out toward the point, exposed to the big waters of the bay, with the geese and few puddle duck decoys that we'd brought inside the cove, downwind a bit and fairly tight to the bank. I didn't want them to be in the way of the divers as they came to the decoys. After all, that is the reason we'd gone to this much trouble. Geese and any puddle ducks would be icing on the cake. I thought our rig looked pretty good, so I eased the boat down the bank a couple hundred yards and stuck it in a small gut. I don't like hiding the boat downwind, but in this case, there was no other viable option. Walking back to the makeshift blind, I admired how unobtrusive our hide for the day was. We blended in with the natural surroundings nicely. As I settled into the blind, I checked the time. We had twenty minutes until legal shooting time. After pouring a cup of coffee, I loaded the Browning. It was game time.

God has a way of truly messing with hunters. Show him your plan, and he'll laugh in your face. He was having a ball with us on this day. With all the talk of the thousands of divers that populated the area, we strained our eyes looking bayward. Expecting redheads and lesser scaup, we were caught by surprise when five baldpates came into view. Though we fired four shots, they escaped, unscathed. We were ready for the next pair that seemed to just materialize over the decoys. Instinct took over. The drake felt the wrath of the humpback and fell among the goose decoys. Catching the wind in its wings, the hen banked sharply away from us. No second shot was possible. We quickly walked out and brought the puddler decoys closer to our blind, making our shots much more manageable. It was one of the better moves of the day.

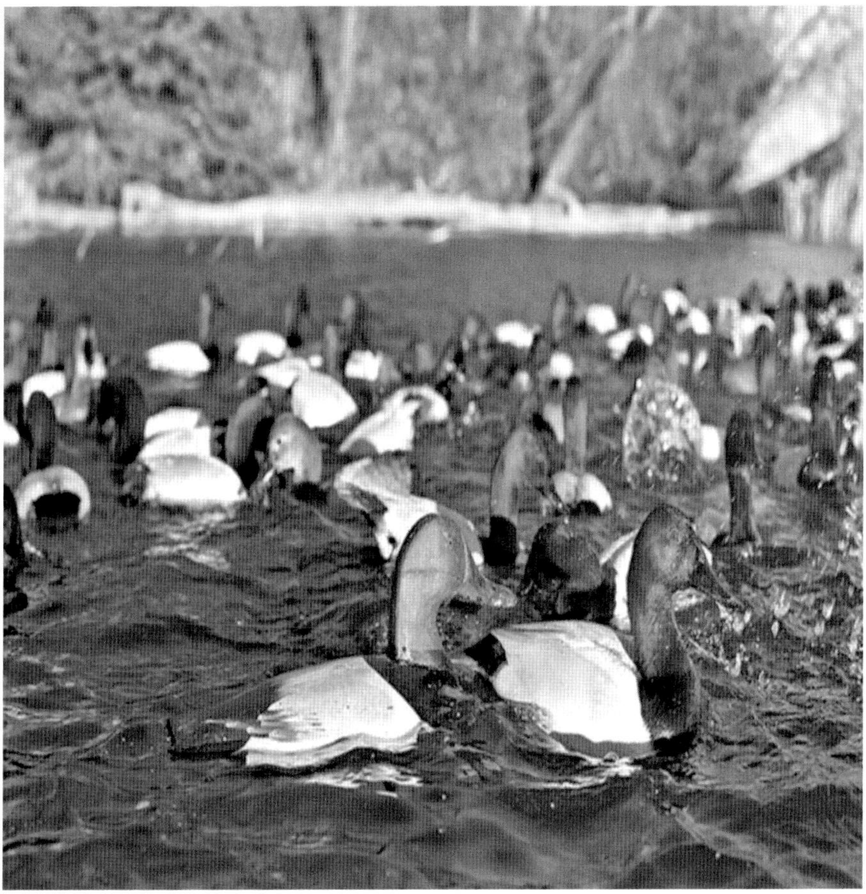

When things are right, canvasbacks will pile into the decoys without hesitation. The handmade block in this picture is overwhelmed by its feathered friends. *Paul Bramble photo.*

For the first hour, we were blessed with baldpates. The largest flock that gave us an opportunity numbered not more than fifteen. We had numerous pairs and threes that committed fully. Shooting in such small bunches enabled us to make a pile rather quickly. It consisted of mostly widgeons, with a few pintails and black ducks sprinkled in for good measure. As the tide began to rise, the divers that we had heard about began to make an appearance.

Singles and pairs began to skirt the outside of our decoys. The first diver to join the party was a kamikaze hen canvasback. It settled in without circling. We let it swim among the decoys until it was startled by a single shot that placed another black duck feet up just ten yards from us. The hen skittered off to the far side of the spread and sat back down. It was safe for now. We were in quest of bull cans.

We saw them coming from the back side of Smith Island. The flock of fifty or so cans flew in broad, long lines just over the tops of the white-capping waves as they made their way toward us. When they reached a distance of about one hundred yards from our decoys, we saw what we came all this way to see. All at once, the entire flock hiked up in the air, suddenly gaining altitude. We just grinned at each other, having seen this play before. Now flying at a height of thirty yards, the fifty feathered bullets swept over the decoys without breaking stride. On pass number two, they were locked and committed. We were ready. Trying to pick out a bull-necked drake, my bead found the closest bird. As I squeezed the trigger, the bird crumpled, along with two behind it. The second shot claimed another fat drake. Shot number three was fired just because I had one left. They'd long since made their departure when that trigger was pulled a third time. Admittedly, I was a little giddy.

As we began to walk out to pick up our prizes, eight redheads cut around the point and settled in among the decoys. We crawled in the back of the blind as these eight realized that they had really screwed up. They formed a tight bunch as we got to our guns. They had turned into the wind preparing for a quick departure. Six shots rang out from our guns in quick succession. Expecting to see most of the eight bobbing in the decoys, we stood with mouths agape watching the entire eight fly off—no cripples, no dead, none injured. It was almost as if they were ghosts in the decoys.

The mix of birds that we had claimed on this day was impressive. Baldpates, sprig tails, blacks, a stray toe-clipped mallard, cans, redheads, bluebills and a token bufflehead collected by collateral damage lay across the center seat of the scow. As the tide began to turn, we decided that we'd shot

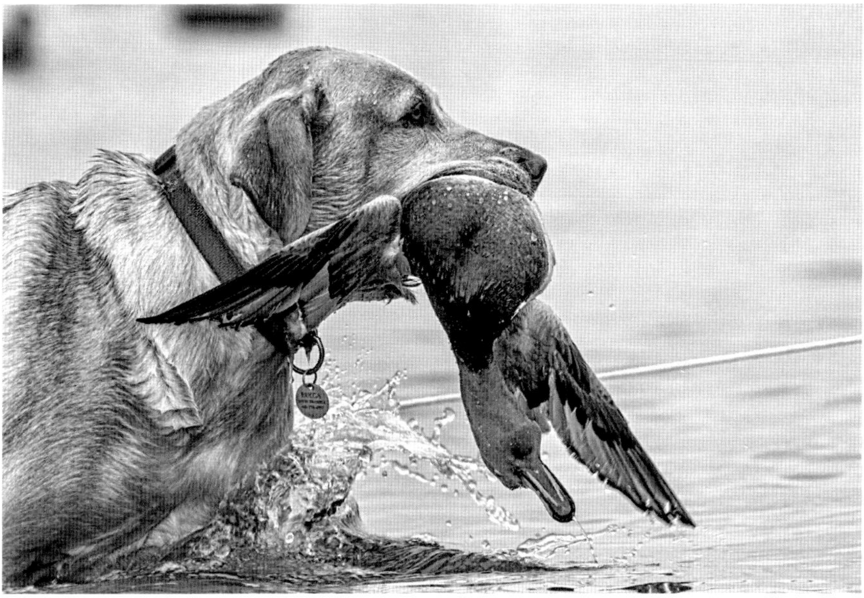

The shallow, grassy flats near South Marsh Island are a natural habitat for redheads. Bucca made another outstanding retrieve on this Tangier Sound bird. *Paul Bramble photo.*

enough and that it was time to head to the barn. Somehow, the trip home wasn't as stressful as the trip over to the island. Somehow, the sunshine and a good morning's shoot can have that effect on a hunter.

We probably should have stayed to enjoy the day's hunting to its fullest, but we were out of coffee and Copenhagen. Sometimes, you just got to know when it's time to pull the plug.

GOOSE HUNTING BONANZA

Located between the Bonanza Restaurant and the Pocomoke High School, there was a piece of farmland that was the best goose field we'd ever seen. On a daily basis, hundreds, if not thousands, of geese fell into the field. Wind, sunshine, rain or warm or cold weather didn't seem to hinder their desire to get onto that plot of land. Too many times to count, we just sat on the tailgate watching geese, drinking beer and wishing we could be set up in there just once. Having asked permission several times in the past, we knew the answer was no.

Two things are certain in this life: time passes and things change. Sitting in the shop in Sanford eating pork chop sandwiches after an early morning teal hunt, we began to hatch a plan for the afternoon. The field came up in conversation. Buddy Glogovic brought up the subject—apparently, the land had sold with plans for development. He knew the new owner and called for permission immediately. Just like that, we were in. We'd just been granted access to the field of our dreams.

Our elation fell to despair as we found that it was located inside the city limits of Pocomoke. Though hunting is not prohibited, discharge of a firearm is illegal within the city limits. To overcome this obstacle, we would have to stand in front of the Pocomoke city council and get special permission. The next meeting was on Wednesday. We had four days to line it up. Work began immediately at coffeehouses and breakfast joints around town. Things were looking good for us, but the city manager was hard to read. With our checkered past in relation to waterfowl hunting, it was decided that Buddy

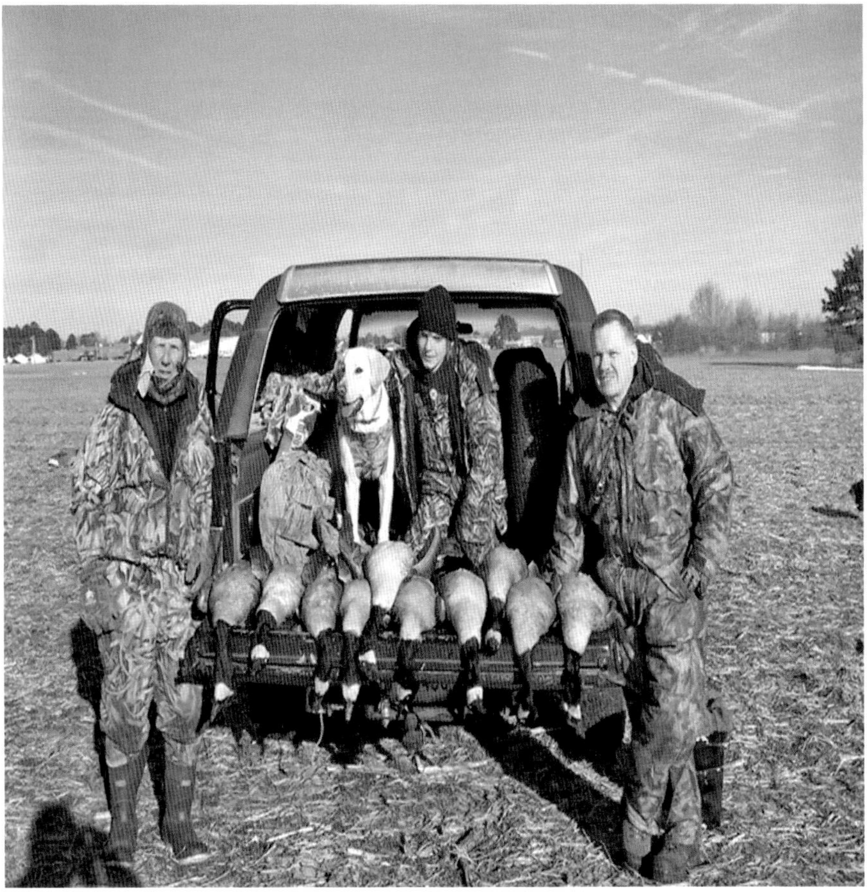

From left to right: Butch Thomas, Max, Hunter Marshall and Buddy Glogovics joined me for a memorable hunt in the Bonanza field. After watching it for years, we were treated to three years of unbelievable goose hunting before the field succumbed to development. *C.L. Marshall photo.*

would be our representative. He was a well-liked local business owner with only one minor skirmish with the Department of Natural Resources.

Now Glogovic was a rare bird. He was a constant worrier and probably could have been the poster child for attention deficit disorder. Each of these traits worked to make him the person he was, and we loved him for it. Before the council meeting, we met at the Upper Deck. He was a bundle of nerves. Four Crown and gingers later, he seemed to be more under control and well schooled on his role. He performed flawlessly. There were a few restrictions, but the council gave us permission.

The field was cut corn. Since it was just a few days until Thanksgiving, we scrambled to get our game in order. Fashioning a blind from bales of hay, with cornstalks as siding, things were progressing nicely. It would be a warm abode, well concealed, with room for four. A small doggie hut was pegged on the highway side of the blind. We made a removable roof that provided cover from descending birds and kept the weather off our decoys. Our collection of decoys was fairly motley, but they'd have to work. Saturday would be our first trip to the mother lode. I hadn't been this excited in years.

The morning went as expected, with a steady stream of geese dropping into our decoys. Limits were achieved quickly. By 8:00 a.m., we were sitting in Market Street Deli eating scrapple, egg and cheese sandwiches while patrons inquired about the "shooting" across from the high school. We continued to bang on them throughout the year. Before school, kids would sit in the high school parking lot and watch us bust 'em. Friends would sit in the Bonanza parking lot and hustle into the blind when one gunner's limit was met. The "two bird shuffle" became the norm. Roll into the blind, whack a pair of geese and roll out. Things were going better than we had planned.

The season was coming to an end. As usual, the best weather of the year came in the last week. Heavy snow north of us, cold weather and strong northwest winds brought us wave after wave of new geese. On the last Saturday of the season, the wind and falling snow made for a picture-perfect gunning day. Most folks just laid in on this day, but we had other plans.

Looking to my left, I saw the usual suspects. The father-and-son team of Butch and Anthony Thomas and Buddy had agreed to spend the last morning of the season looking for a few limits of geese. Just a few minutes after legal shooting time, we were halfway there. As the sun broke over the eastern horizon, we needed just two more. We all agreed that we'd shoot into just one more flock. With that agreement, a flock of forty crossed the highway and then dropped below the tree line. There was no doubt about their intention. Ours was never in doubt either.

As it was to be our last flock of year, I wanted it to be just right. If it wasn't, then we'd pass until it got right. About one hundred yards from the decoys, fighting the wind, the flock began to gain altitude. Some hunters might have panicked, but we sat tight. At that new altitude, they circled once and then collected themselves and began to settle perfectly into the slot. I momentarily lost track of the birds closest to us and continued to watch the geese at the end of the flock. A dozen or so were walking in the decoys when I called the shot. Four guns spoke in unison as a path was cut through the incoming birds. Singles were picked off with subsequent shots. Max, Anthony's yellow

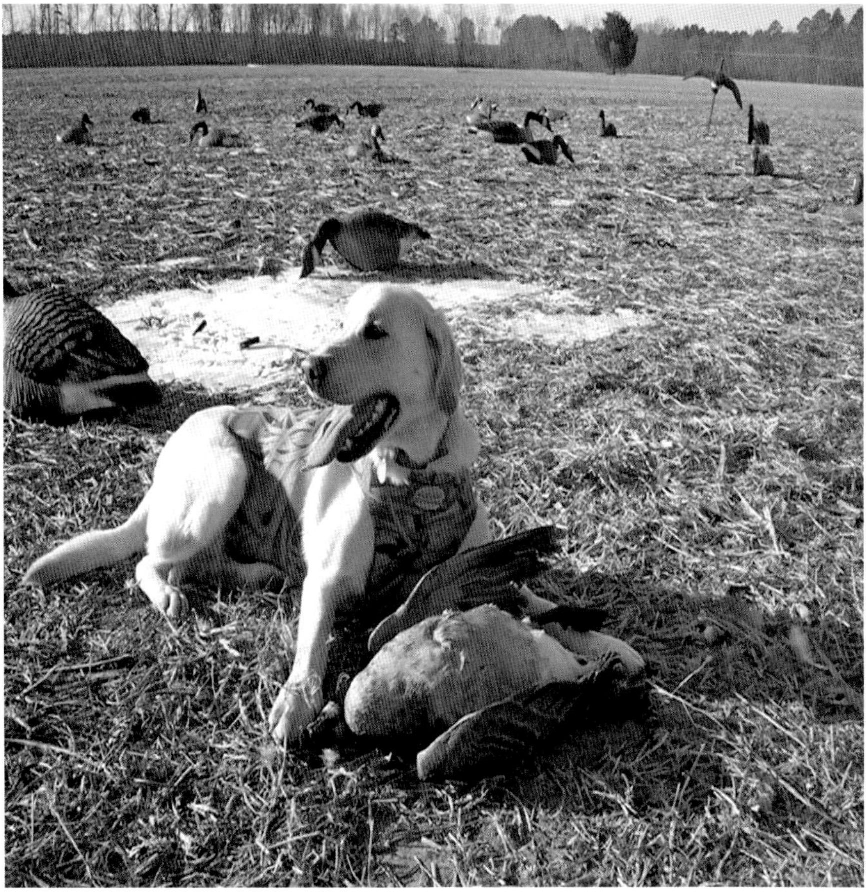

Max takes a break from a rather busy morning of hauling geese back to the blind. His return trip with a goose in tow was often quicker than his outbound trip. *C.L. Marshall photo.*

lab, was off with the first shots. As we began to dispatch cripples, he was back with his second retrieve. His third pickup was a rather large goose, with still a little life left in him. On the way back, the goose squirmed and blocked his eyesight. Rolling back full bore, Max was knocking down decoys like bowling pins. With his limited eyesight, he failed to stop at the blind, striking the side of the hay bales at full force. Two bales, the goose and Max spilled across the snow-covered field. He was off again. There was no need for hand signals, whistles or commands. Geese were lying everywhere.

Butch, Anthony and I were busy handling cripples. Max was still picking up the dead. Buddy was talking to himself, just walking in tight circles mumbling that we all were going to jail. Tossing a pair back toward the blind, Butch observed Buddy's condition. I'd asked Buddy to go get his truck so we could pick up the decoys and the birds and break down the blind. He just couldn't get himself in gear.

"Buddy! Buddy!" Butch yelled atop the chaos. Finally, Buddy broke out of his trance and looked up.

"You need to calm down. Take one of your pills and get one for Max, too. Then go get the truck. We have to get outta here."

With that, we began to rein in the chaos that we created. He got the message, avoided the road on the way back and had his red Ford V10 rolling across corn stubble at a deliberate rate. We were picked up, cleaned up and rolled up in short order. Once he focused, he was a machine. Hay bales, decoys, geese, spent gun shells and equipment were quickly and neatly stacked in the bed of his truck.

We had looked on this field as something unattainable. Working through the obstacles that would have stopped many made the journey as memorable as the outcome. The memories that we shared on that piece of dirt will last a lifetime. It was subsequently sold to another developer, and just enough houses were built on it to prevent further hunting activity. Now the land is about half the size that it was in our heyday, but geese still annually populate it on a regular basis. No one else will have that experience on that field. Each time I ride by it, I can't help but think of the good memories made there.

I'd give up a lot for the four of us to share that hay bale blind again. Unfortunately, that will never happen. Though times change and people pass on, the sight of the geese coming and going in that field has been a constant reminder of what was and of what will never be again.

THE MORE, THE MERRIER

As is the case more often than not, the last few days of the 2011 season were marked by a cold snap. Temperatures in the single digits and a lack of any appreciable wind translated into a thick layer of ice over the creeks and tributaries of the Pocomoke Sound. A falling tide would provide some access to the multitude of puddle ducks that had been pushed south to us. Rising tides would only fill these smallish creeks with slush and piled up ice, rendering boat use dangerous for occupants and equipment.

The season had been quite good, and this colder weather at season's end had provided the icing on a pretty damn good cake. Looking at the last day of the season on the horizon, we began to lay plans to shoot an air hole just inside the mouth of Holden's Creek. The swift-running current rarely froze and had been open throughout this arctic event. Mallards, blacks, widgeon and teal had been coming and going to this area since the freeze began. The numbers steadily rose each day. As the temperature rose into the balmy teens during the midday sun of the day before the planned hunt, we fashioned a blind out of the available materials. Saltwater bushes, reeds and sea oats were arranged in a form that would hide four to five hunters in the coming day. All indications pointed to a good shoot to end the year.

Meeting in the predawn hours down on the Hall farm, five of us prepared for the last hunt of the year. We had a good group that would provide a load of fun during this day's hunt. Benny Hall Jr. and I had hunted quite a bit together over the years. We were joined by one of Ben's farmhands and our mutual friend Accomack County deputy sheriff Shane Childress. With

Shane tagging along, we'd have to play by the rules. My son Parker rounded out our five.

Just as we were preparing to roll out, my phone rang. Anthony Thomas and his Saxis Islander father, Butch, had tried to bust out through the ice on Messongo Creek. Not able to make it happen, they called to see what I had going. They were invited to tag along, on the promise that they would bring his yellow dog, Max. My golden was out with a cut pad, and the addition of a dog would make things much, much easier. Our party, inclusive of Max, grew to eight.

Because the lot was private land, we wouldn't have to worry about a whole lot. The frozen field took the worry out of parking. We were well off the road and out of the sight of prying eyes. A short walk through a sliver of woods and across about one hundred yards of frozen marsh brought us to our crudely constructed blind. Ben and I handled the decoy chores while the balance of our party took to providing an addition to our blind. The tide was low at the beginning of the incoming. We placed our dozen mallard and black duck decoys just inside the point on the far side of the creek. There they would be unaffected by the incoming ice. Eight or so mallard field decoys were stuck up on the exposed sandbar. They'd have to be monitored as the tide began its rise. The spread looked alive in the true north wind.

The shooting began as Ben and I were wading off the sandbar. Parker and Shane pulled two fat mallards out of a flock of four that tried to sneak in from up the creek. Max had them delivered back to Anthony by the time I reached the makeshift blind. Ben and I reached the hide to find our guns uncased and loaded and birds working the decoys. The earlier shots had gotten things moving on the creek. The sky was full of ducks. It was a very welcomed sight. Mallards, twenty-five in total, made a high pass around our setup. These were not local birds, as evidenced by their behavior. They were new arrivals and looking for a place to rest. The second pass provided the opportunity we were looking for. With the majority of them slowing greatly as they crossed the decoys, there was no need to call the shot. The eight of us moved in unison and unleashed hell on the twenty birds that were in and around the decoys. They were falling everywhere. Max was bringing them back as fast as his legs would let him. Ben and I walked out on the exposed sandbar and began handling the crippled fowl. We'd done well, picking up eleven, but we all were in agreement that we thought we'd done better than that.

The next hour was one that waterfowl hunting memories are made of. It wasn't just for quality and quantity of birds that continued to attempt to join our party. It wasn't just the hits and misses. It wasn't just the good shots and good retrieves that we got to witness. Rather, it was a unique combination of each of these and being able to share it with good people who appreciated what we were involved in. All was right with the world.

Then Shane's phone rang.

Perched on the creek bank, a measured 236 yards by laser, is a Cape Cod–style home now occupied by a "come here" from Baltimore. Apparently, the rash of shooting awakened some rather unpleasant memories from his prior homestead in the city. His repeated calls to the sheriff's department complaining about our activities had been averted to this point. We were of adequate distance from his home according to Virginia law. We were on private land, and our hunt was perfectly legal. Being nearly upwind from our location, our shooting would have been heard from his home but shouldn't have been too awfully loud. His complaint that we had shot his house was one that required investigation. Apparently, this fellow was having a bad day and wanted to ruin ours. I guess he just couldn't stand to see us having fun.

Knowing that Shane was in the area, the dispatcher called him to update him on the situation and asked if he wanted to respond. He stated that a car should be dispatched, and he'd meet the responding officer at the house. Leaving his shotgun, he began the trek up to the complainants' house. We just kept shooting.

The wind shifted from north to northeast. The rising tide was now allowing ice to slide across the once exposed sandbar, which endangered our spread of field decoys stuck in the sand. As Shane departed, I elected to take advantage of the situation and relocate those decoys closer to our blind and out of harm's way. As I began to handle this task, I noticed that Max was getting a bit agitated. Normally a really laidback dog, Max now verged on unruly. This was very odd. Anthony's stern commands fell on deaf ears as Max ultimately couldn't stand it anymore. In spite of the harsh words being hurled his way, Max sprinted down the bank directly into the northeast wind. The shifting wind had apparently brought the scent of a bird lying in the marsh just up the bank. It had to be fetched, and fetch it he did, evidence of a pretty good nose. He delivered a fat black to Anthony's waiting hand.

Shane's return was not greeted by the obvious questions. The grin on his face told the whole story. I can't imagine the old boy's face as a wader-clad, badge-wearing member of the "offending" party strode up to handle his complaint. It was probably one of the more rewarding calls of his career.

We continued to grind on the puddlers, electing to trade our blind for hot coffee and scrapple, egg and cheese sandwiches at Martha's Kitchen. The eight of us sat in that creek point restaurant, sipping coffee and reliving

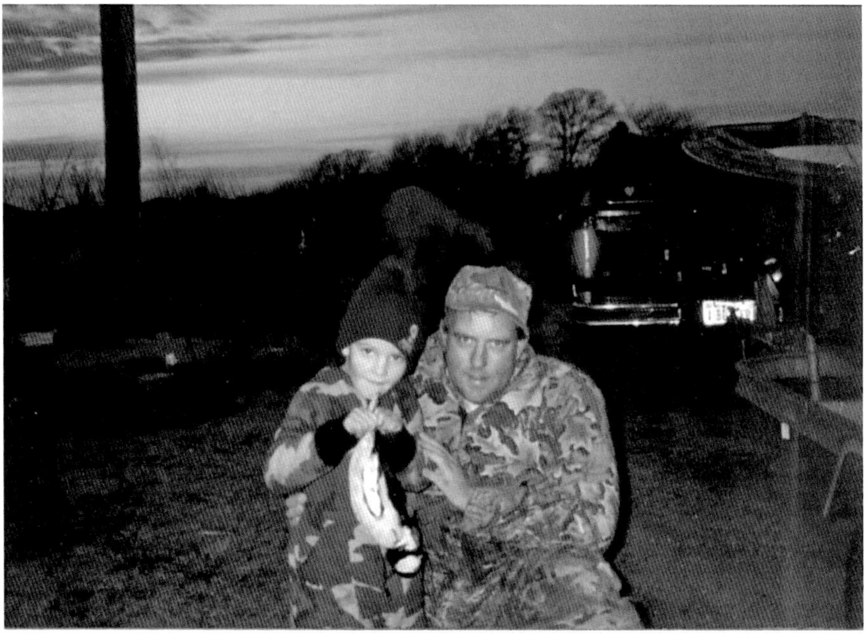

Parker Marshall and I have shared many outstanding experiences afield. One of the most memorable was this bufflehead that he rolled out with his .410. *C.L. Marshall photo.*

the events of the morning. Those who on a regular basis hold court in Martha's couldn't help but sit back and laugh about what had occurred on this morning.

One of the cool things about waterfowl hunting is the decidedly social aspect of it—being able to laugh, talk in a normal tone of voice and, on occasion, chase a fellow hunter around the area. It also offers the opportunity to hunt in complete solitude, alone with our thoughts. That's what makes the sport so appealing. It can be tailored to our individual needs at any given time. It can be flexible, loud and gregarious. This day was all of that and more.

THE PICTURE

It now hangs in my office, and I look directly at it as I begin each day. It has occupied a prominent place in each house and apartment I've lived in. Over the years, it has come to mean many things to me. In the years to come, it will again take on several different meanings.

The twenty- by twenty-four-inch canvas oil painting found its way to me in 1977. It's an original artwork by Grayson Chesser, who lives just up the road in Jenkins Bridge. On the surface, some may say it's just another hunting picture, but closer inspection by one who has chased black ducks for forty years gives it additional meaning. It depicts what every duck hunter aspires to. From a well-built, barely noticeable blind on a shallow tree-lined creek, we see three black ducks committed to the fifteen decoys. The Duxbak canvas–clad hunter, complete with canvas Surrey hat, has risen to the occasion. His humpbacked Browning A5 is shouldered. It is obvious that he is a seasoned hunter. Shots have been fired. The bird to the left is falling with a broken wing and will crash, breast first, into the creek. The second has been rocked, killed instantly, as falling feathers surround the bird in the moment before it begins its descent into the creek. What's left up to the observer is whether or not there's a third shot available. Did the second shot miss? Will he pull on the third duck? His black lab has already broken and is airborne, bounding toward the first falling duck.

In *A Ducks Unlimited Guide to Hunting Dabblers*, Wade Bourne wrote, "When a duck hunter gets it all right, the satisfaction is sublime. When he picks the precise spot, fashions a good blind, sets his decoys to look like live ducks on the water, calls convincingly and makes a clean kill…he has reached a high pinnacle of achievement." This picture embodies all of that.

Black ducks hold a special place in the heart of many hunters. My attraction began as a youngster sitting on the counter at Til Fisher's General Store in my hometown of Sanford. The aggressive attitude toward this species of fowl was bred into us. Listening to the men sitting around the store on a Saturday morning recount the stories of their morning's adventures, it became evident that there was a special place for black ducks in their hearts. I remember one elder statesman of the area expounding his hatred for blacks. He said that all "sporting measures" went out the window when it comes to black ducks. He'd shoot them walking, sleeping, swimming or flying if he had to.

According to local lore, the local population of black ducks would venture over to Michael's Marsh for their formal education. There they would become wise to the ways of the average hunter. Local hunters would go above and beyond the normally accepted methods of covering a blind. Face paint was used in Saxis long before it was made famous by those boys from Monroe, Louisiana. These birds seem to have a sixth sense, picking up on the smallest inkling that something might not be right. They're old and fat. They didn't get that way from being stupid.

As in any story, written or painted, the setting is critical. The lone hunter's perch along a winding creek is sheltered by hardwoods and cypress, both devoid of foliage. Small cedars dot both sides of the creek. The gray, sunless sky imparts the feeling of a cold January morning. The bright orange legs of the quarry dictate that it's late in the Virginia season. These birds are "migrators," the largest and most sought-after quarry for Eastern Shore puddle duck hunters.

Countless times, I've been in that blind. Many times, I've been that hunter. I'll venture there at the most random of times. Each time I mentally transport to that place, it's always with a sense of calm, purpose and thankfulness. As hunters, we relish those times and remember how we felt during the experience more often than how many we killed. Growing older often leads to more reflection. It leads to appreciation for this lifestyle we have chosen.

As for me, when I transport myself to that blind on a reed-covered bayside shoreline, I've still got one left in the chamber and plan on bringing down that third bird.

THEN AND NOW

Watching my son and one of his friends chase down a crippled goose, I sat wondering if he'd run the boat out on the flats to jump the eight hundred or so geese that were rafted up out there. I voiced my concern and sincere hope that he would avoid the temptation. My gunning partner for the day, Steve Barnes, simply stated that the geese would jump and reset farther out in the bay. The next statement he made set me to thinking. "I had to go through nineteen to get to forty-five," he quipped.

It made me think about the many changes that we've seen in the last forty years of gunning. The exuberance of a filled bag has been replaced by the total experience of the hunt. A single good retrieve now is extremely satisfying. Watching those who began their hunting career with me develop into skilled hunters in their own right is routinely gratifying. Seeing "green" hunters work through their issues, overcome their mistakes and grow into responsible stewards of the sport is something that won't easily be overshadowed. Several factors have encouraged teenagers to venture afield of late. The mainstreaming of country music and the televised hunts of its more popular names has piqued the interest of some. Many others were exposed via *Duck Dynasty*. Missing are the twenty-five- to thirty-five-year-old hunters. It appears as though the Gen X folks just couldn't be bothered with it. It requires a little work.

Camo has gone mainstream. Gone are the days of third-generation hand-me-downs and Duxbak waxed-canvas wear. These days, there are camouflage patterns designed to match just about every woodland and marsh in the United States. There's camo to match the moon, water, sky

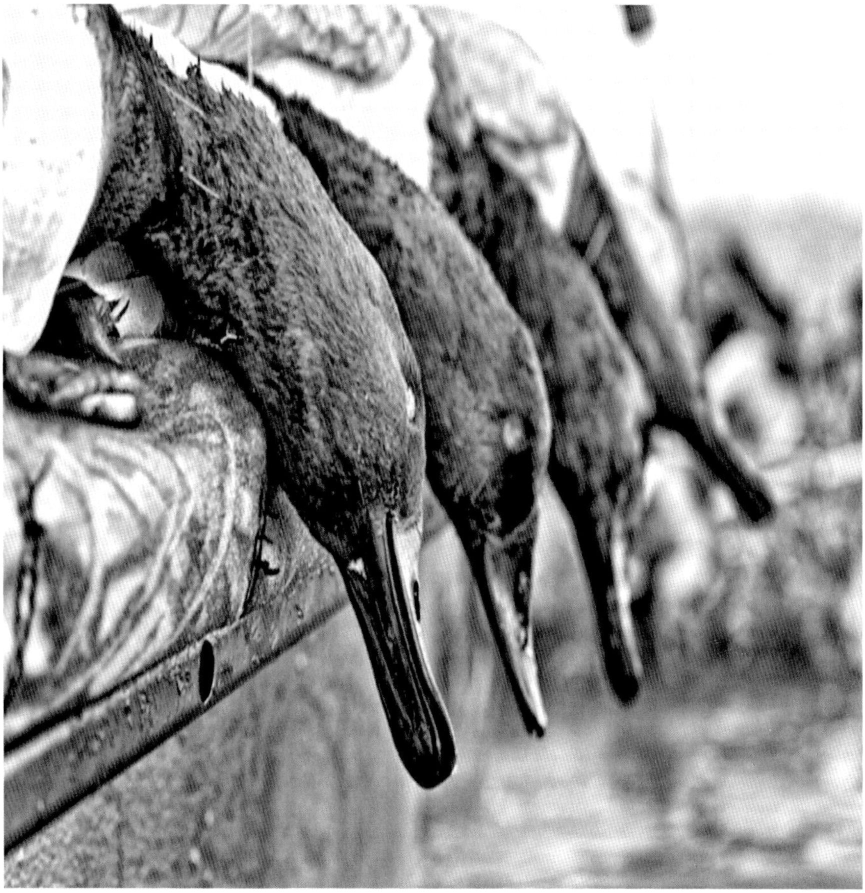

Limits of canvasbacks signal that a hunter has learned the art of waterfowl hunting well. For many reasons, they still are called the king of ducks. *Paul Bramble photo.*

and everything in between. According to the manufacturers, without it there is little chance of success.

Most hunters owned three guns. Usually, the first was a shotgun given as a Christmas or birthday present. This was usually followed by a .22 for plinking and small-game hunting. The third was a centerfire rifle usually of .270 or .30-06 for deer hunting. These three weapons were satisfactory for chasing anything from buffleheads to bison. These days, after reading the industry "jack" magazines, one might think it is imperative to own a different firearm for every endeavor. One must have a turkey shotgun for turkey hunting and a different one for waterfowling. That rifle that is used for whitetail hunting certainly won't work on hogs, plains game or close-range elk. The .22 is fine, but by adding a .17 to the arsenal, that squirrel can be tamed at eighty yards. The avid hunter never seems to have enough game-specific weapons.

Access to hunting property has changed drastically and in some ways is prohibitive. There are many public opportunities, and some are better than others. Opportunity to hunt on private land was granted for the asking more often than not in my youth. Often it was offered with a caveat, such as, "Hunt all the ducks you want, just don't mess with my deer," or "Sure you can goose hunt on that farm. Will you bring me a pair if you have any extra?" Local farmers and landowners allowed locals access. That's changed in many cases due to the big-dollar leases paid by the highest bidder. Hunters from metropolitan areas and groups of like-minded individuals pooling their money in hunt clubs have curbed local opportunity. This has resulted in posted signs popping up like daffodils on most fields and blocks of woodland. There ain't much room for local love when there's dollars involved.

When I was growing up, you didn't need a hunting license prior to the age of sixteen. The art was gleaned from parents, friends and listening to the elders while sitting on the counter at Til Fisher's store. It was routine to walk the marshes jump-shooting black ducks at the age of twelve. It was commonplace to see a group of thirteen-year-olds walking down the street with shotguns cradled in their arms. Shells were lead. Cripples were few. Ammo could be purchased by the individual shell. Many times, we'd purchase six or throw our money together and get ten. That was when we were planning a big day or had some ducks using and planned a "crawl down."

Under current law, classes must be taken and a test passed to be eligible to purchase a license. Combined cost of each has added to the prohibitive nature of the sport. Many parents who don't hunt don't see the need to encourage or enable their kids to do so. Imagine the influx of calls to the local police department resulting from a young man walking through downtown Pocomoke with his deer rifle en route to his field on Dividing Creek road. The negative public perception of hunting and firearms is predicated on the actions of the few and has adverse effects on many. Television, newspapers, magazines and radio choose to publicize negative stories. Many suggest bans and mandatory registration of all firearms as the road to social salvation. Such encumbrance on the law-abiding citizenry will have no effect on those who choose to carry out heinous acts. Criminals will find a way to be criminals.

But each of the aforementioned changes is more of the social aspect. Each is representative of the change of thinking about hunting and how this thought process has been altered forever by actions of the irresponsible few. Such external influences have forever changed the sport. But over time, intrinsic changes in

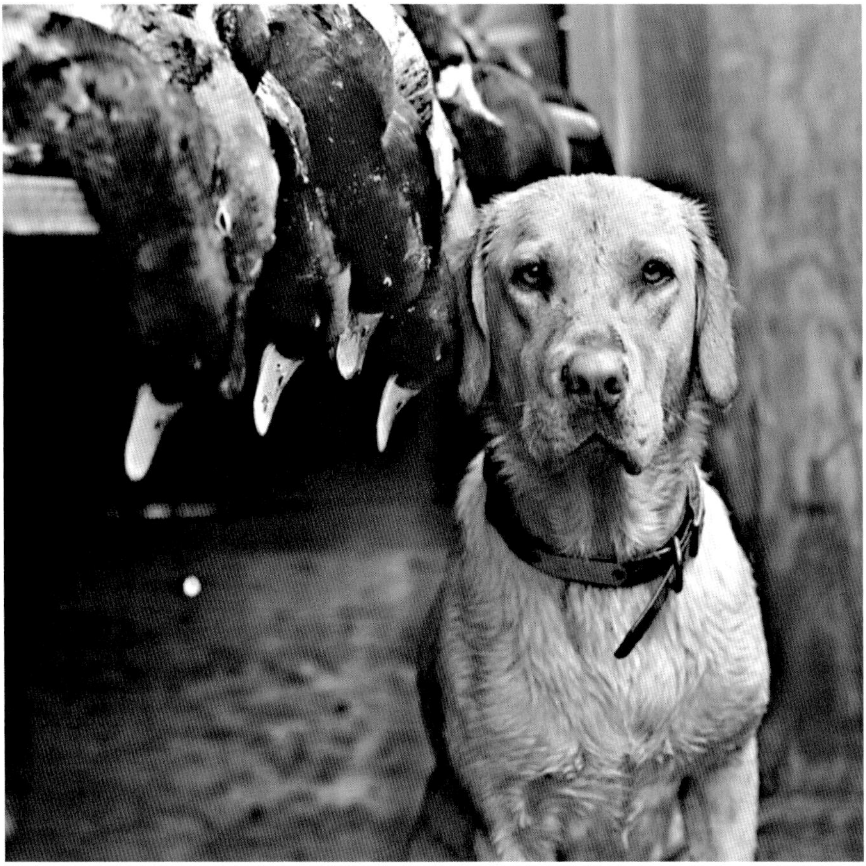

Good gun dogs are possessive of "their" ducks. Cudi had a busy morning and poses with her mixed bag of divers. *Paul Bramble photo*.

each hunter are just as drastic. The road at sixteen was very different from the one I tread at fifty-two. The desire is still there, but it has taken a different form. Two shots on cupped, committed, landing gear–down geese are more satisfying than pass shooting a dozen. Though I still enjoy the occasional bufflehead hunt, it's now the exception rather than the norm. It's usually a twenty-gauge hunt, drakes only, and serves as more of a training exercise for the dog. Geese, puddlers and big divers now occupy my time.

Progressing through the recognized five stages of the hunter, it's quite difficult to witness those coming behind me suffer through the same trials and tribulations that most my age have endured. Experience is the greatest teacher, and in successful duck hunting, there's no substitute for it. They will all learn in their own way.

TURNABOUT IS FAIR PLAY IN ROCK HALL

As the 2011 season wore on, it became obvious that if we were going to have any success at all, we were going to have to have some weather. The November split was pretty decent as we picked on a pretty steady diet of summer ducks. It was shaping up to be that kind of year. We got what we were looking for around Christmas as temperatures plummeted.

With the frigid weather came new birds. The Saxis Wildlife Management Area became inundated with black ducks, widgeon and teal. The open waters of the Chesapeake supplied us with steady shooting on cans, redheads and blue bills. It was going very, very nicely. The numbers of Canada geese that we were holding was truly amazing but paled in comparison to what was happening just ninety miles to the north.

One of my college buddies and a group of his friends had come together to lease a few farms in the Chestertown area. They'd invited me up for a couple days in late December, with the stipulation that I'd provide dinner. I felt that they were adequately satisfied with the slabs of black sea bass that I brought. They got it pan fried or grilled with a balsamic glaze, served with fresh collards, mashed redskin potatoes and sweet potato biscuits. There were no complaints. We shared a pit on the King Farm, just outside Rock Hall, Maryland, where we shot a four-man limit on consecutive mornings. We were living high on the hog.

The cold weather layered the bay waters off Saxis with a thick layer of ice. Though we were able to break through it for some very good hunting early in the freeze, it became impassible for our outboards soon afterward.

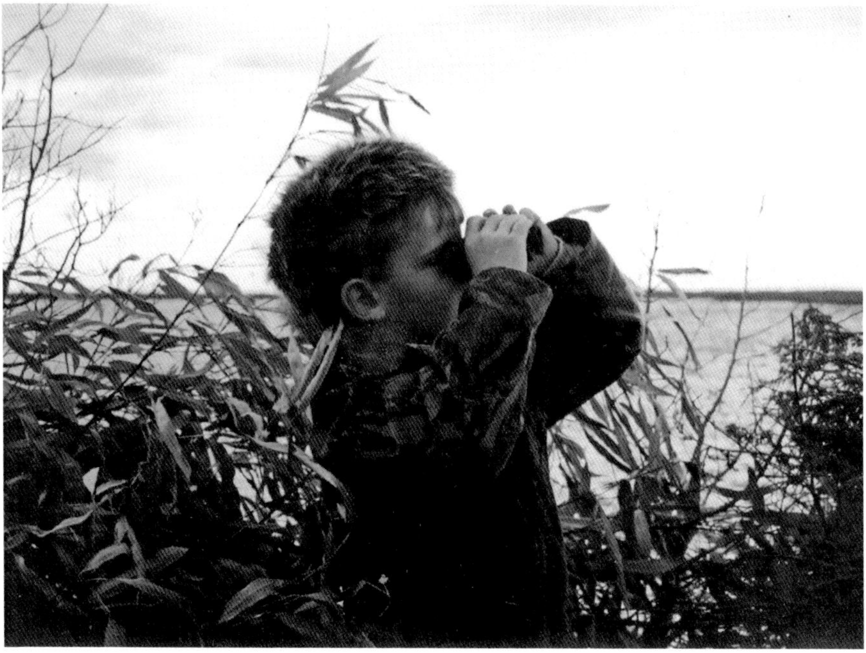

Hunter Marshall watches a small flock of swans make their way across Back Bay. *C.L. Marshall photo.*

We were frozen in. The first couple days of it were spent riding, glassing and hoping for a way out. It wasn't going to happen. We just hung it up for a couple days—that is, until I got a call from David Arris, aka D.A., aka "the Big Chinaman."

Now, this fella is a true anomaly. Labeled by a youngster in a convenience store early one morning as "the biggest Chinaman I've ever seen," he's a ball of energy. His brother was coming in from San Francisco, and his primary hunting area of Back Bay/Knott's Island was locked in with ice as well. I received his call early one Wednesday morning, and we discussed our options. The only possible opportunity we had to take his brother hunting was to find some open water, and the best option would be on the seaside near Gargathy. There the ramps are fairly close to the inlet and the current runs strong, and a couple years prior, we'd stuck a blind over there. I agreed to scout in preparation for a Saturday hunt.

Two days before our pending hunt, I towed the boat over to Gargatha. The temperature gauge read nine degrees. I was very familiar with the area. In the summer month, I ply its waters for clams, oysters and flounder. Many teenage nights have been spent on the beach fishing for sharks and just doing what kids do on the Eastern Shore after the sun goes down. Fortunately, I didn't have to launch the boat. The salty seaside water was flowing freely, and I was pleased to see it. Through the binoculars, I could see under the beach and along the intercoastal waterway that I would have ample places to hunt come Saturday. Sipping my hot coffee, I turned the truck back toward home.

On the appointed Saturday, I met the Arris party at the ramp. David, his father and his brother climbed aboard the scow, and we were quickly off in the darkness. Though familiar with the area, I idled along slowly in the twelve-degree air. The northwest winds had already begun to pick up, now gusting at up to fifteen miles per hour. With sunup, they would certainly reach twenty to twenty-five. Our spot for the day would be cold but promised to provide a good day's shoot.

The blind was in better shape than I thought it would be. Since we hadn't visited it in over two years, it took a little bushing with whatever we could scrounge, and it looked pretty good. The best find was a full sheet of plywood that we used as the back of the blind, a welcomed addition to provide shelter from the wind's bite. We settled in, fired up the propane heater and readied ourselves for what was sure to come. It didn't take long for things to get going.

First light brought seven black ducks to our decoys. They were followed by a steady stream of buffleheads (narkels), lawn darts (mergansers) and a pair of geese. From the north came a pile of brant. It looked like maybe

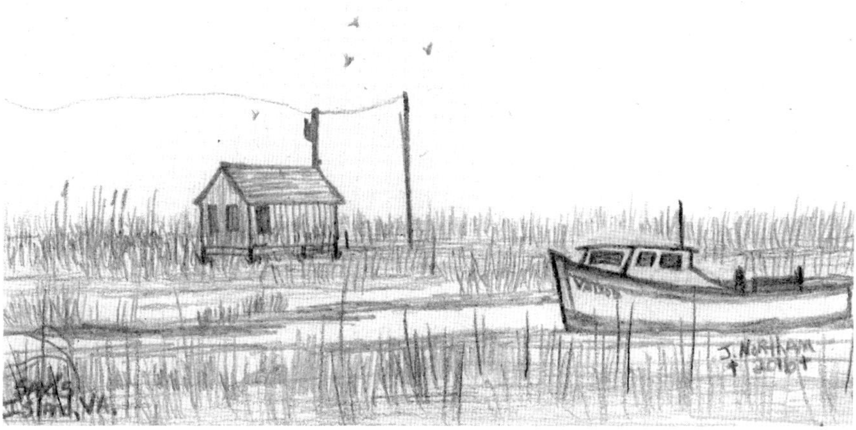

twenty or so. A few brant-like sounds from the Eastern Shoreman drew their attention to the decoys, and they were on a string.

"Brant, from the left!" I whispered urgently to our party.

"Are they good to eat?" David shot back.

"Chincoteaguer's love 'em. Cut 'em!" was my reply.

I knew better than to shoot. The three of them cut hell in 'em. As expected, I picked up our limit of eight, which concluded our day. After the dekes were picked up, we made our way back to the truck. They had a good day and took the birds, and we went our separate ways. Two days later, I accepted the invitation for another trip to Chestertown. I was told to make some soup.

When I arrived, right at dinnertime, with a pot of rockfish chowder, there was a fowl stench in the air. Placing the soup on the stove, I couldn't find the source of the odor. Pouring a three-finger glass of Maker's Mark, I took a seat on the couch to plan the coming day. David and Todd were bringing something out of the kitchen.

Served on toast points, with a little tomato, was grilled brant. My god, it was awful. It smelled bad and tasted worse. Those two, who had realized the game's poor table quality since our last hunt, had make a point by getting back at me for my little white lie the prior Saturday.

I've yet to shoot another one.

ABOUT THE AUTHOR

C.L Marshall grew up near Saxis Island, Virginia, and began plying its waters for fish and fowl at an early age. C.L. received much of his hunting education from the locals of that area who have earned an outlaw reputation with a rich and checkered duck hunting past. This influence made for some very unique situations involving conservation officers charged with thwarting such outlaw ways.

As a former sports editor for the *Eastern Shore News*, editor of the *Mid-Atlantic Fisherman* and cofounder of *Shore Golf* magazine, Marshall has received numerous awards for his unique outdoor writing style. His most recent release, *A Taste of Eastern Shore Living*, revealed the culinary secrets of Delmarva kitchens utilizing locally available wildfowl, fish and game.

Chesapeake Bay Duck Hunting Tales' thirty short stories show the transformation of the author from a wide-ranging outlaw hunter to a more mature, appreciative steward of our waterfowl populations. If you are a hunter, or know one, it's a journey you're sure to enjoy.